70 CLASSIC RECIPES FROM
Bulgaria, Romania
Croatia & Slovenia

70 CLASSIC RECIPES FROM
Bulgaria, Romania Croatia & Slovenia

DELICIOUS, AUTHENTIC, TRADITIONAL DISHES FROM AN UNDISCOVERED CUISINE, SHOWN IN 270 PHOTOGRAPHS

LESLEY CHAMBERLAIN AND TRISH DAVIES

H H
HERMES
HOUSE

This edition is published by Hermes House, an imprint of Anness Publishing Ltd,
Hermes House, 88–89 Blackfriars Road, London SE1 8HA;
tel. 020 7401 2077; fax 020 7633 9499

www.hermeshouse.com; www.annesspublishing.com

If you like the images in this book and would like to investigate using them for publishing,
promotions or advertising, please visit our website www.practicalpictures.com for more
information.

Publisher: Joanna Lorenz
Editor: Margaret Malone
Photography: Dave Jordan
Styling: Marion McLornan
Food for Photography: Sara Lewis, assisted by Julie Beresford
Illustrators: Angela Wood (artworks) and David Cook (maps)
Editorial Reader: Joy Wotton
Production Controller: Claire Rae
Picture credits: p7 Magnum Photos

ETHICAL TRADING POLICY

Because of our ongoing ecological investment programme, you, as our customer, can have the
pleasure and reassurance of knowing that a tree is being cultivated on your behalf to naturally
replace the materials used to make the book you are holding. For further information about
this scheme, go to www.annesspublishing.com/trees

Previously published as *The Balkan Cookbook*

NOTES

For all recipes, quantities are given in both metric and imperial measures and, where
appropriate, in standard cups and spoons. Follow one set of measures, but not
a mixture, because they are not interchangeable.

Standard spoon and cup measures are level. 1 tsp = 5ml, 1 tbsp = 15ml, 1 cup = 250ml/8fl oz.

Australian standard tablespoons are 20ml. Australian readers should use 3 tsp
in place of 1 tbsp for measuring small quantities.

American pints are 16fl oz/2 cups. American readers should use 20fl oz/2.5 cups
in place of 1 pint when measuring liquids.

Electric oven temperatures in this book are for conventional ovens. When using a fan oven, the
temperature will probably need to be reduced by about 10–20°C/20–40°F. Since ovens vary,
you should check with your manufacturer's instruction book
for guidance.

Medium (US large) eggs are used unless otherwise stated.

Main front cover image shows *Onion and Fish Casserole* – for recipe, see page 54

PUBLISHER'S NOTE

CONTENTS

INTRODUCTION

The southern portion of Eastern Europe lies between the Adriatic and Black Seas, a group of countries commonly referred to as the Balkans. In this fascinating region, the hearty German and Austro-Hungarian cooking styles to the north-west overlap with more exotic culinary traditions borrowed from Turkey and the Near East, plus an occasional Russian influence. The result is a varied cuisine that takes full advantage of the diverse vegetables and herbs grown in the region and tends to be spicier than more northern cooking styles.

QUALITY INGREDIENTS
The accent in all the region's cooking is on flavour and quality. Typical dishes based on everyday ingredients include stuffed cabbage leaves, peppers or aubergines, or raw salad vegetables served with grilled or spit-roasted chicken. Excellent bread, dairy products, fruit, pork and fish also figure

prominently in the diet. Wine is being produced in increasing quantities, following ancient traditions as well as new methods.

EXOTIC INFLUENCES
The Turkish influence is most apparent in Romania and Bulgaria, where traditional starters called *meze* include tomatoes, peppers, olives, baked aubergines, bean salads, cheese and ham as well as European sausage. Bulgarian *pasterma*, which is dried beef often combined with paprika, and Dalmatian *prsut*, a dark smoked ham like Italian prosciutto, count among the highlights of the *meze* table. Yogurt, pickled cucumbers, vegetables and such fish delicacies as *tarama* are also popular.

Connoisseurs of Turkish cooking will also recognize the Romanian speciality *placinta* and its Bulgarian and Serbian counterparts. These flaky pastry pies filled with meat or cheese, or cheese and spinach, are usually served hot after *meze*.

FRESH VEGETABLES AND FRUIT
Vegetables are grown in abundance in domestic gardens and allotments and are on sale fresh in markets everywhere. Ranging from all the many northern root crops to the southern summer crops of aubergines, peppers, tomatoes, courgettes and okra, they figure prominently in most dishes. Among the many fruits grown are apricots, peaches and watermelons.

When Bulgarian cooks get to work incorporating vegetables into casseroles, with or without meat, the results are memorable. These oven-baked dishes, called *gyuvech* in Bulgarian, *ghiveci* in Romanian and *djuvec* in Serbian, are named after the earthenware pots in which they are slowly cooked. Bulgarians are also fond of rice dishes, which typically incorporate courgettes or spinach. *Shopska* salad, a typical first course for lunch or dinner in Bulgaria, is made of generous chunks of tomatoes, cucumber and onion dressed with yogurt.

Left: The countries lying between the Adriatic Sea and the Black Sea offer some of the most tasty and surprising food of Eastern Europe. With influences as varied as Turkey and Greece in the south-east, Italy to the west and the rich traditions of the Central European countries, this is hardly surprising.

PRODUCE FROM SEA AND RIVER

Great waterways, including the Danube River, pass through or wash the fringes of the Balkan countries so a strong tradition in fish cookery comes as no surprise. Plates of small fried fish, eaten with chunks of white bread and washed down with wine or cold beer are a delight wherever they are found.

Romania's oldest recipes are for stews and simple grills using the once plentiful river fish of the Danube river and its delta, such as grey mullet and carp, and catfish from the Black Sea. Many of these recipes have been adapted in this book for use with more readily available meaty fish such as tuna, marlin and shark.

Good fish are still abundant along the Dalmatian seaboard of Croatia and Serbia. It is hard to know which to rate higher: a plate of mixed fried fish from the Adriatic or a fish soup with wine and garlic, rosemary and olive oil.

MEAT DISHES

Balkan cooks have excellent ways with meat, whether plain, grilled and served with sour pickles as in Romania, cooked as kebabs or casseroled with vegetables in the Bulgarian style.

Romanians and Croatians also specialize in delicious, barbecued, spicy meatballs of pork or mixed pork and beef served with peppers preserved in olive oil.

Pork and fried chips is an easily prepared but reliable dish found everywhere, although with a little more effort the meat may be simmered in beer. Pork fat is widely used for cooking in Romania, where a family living on the edge of a small town might well keep a pig for its own use.

Lamb is most popular in Bulgaria, where it is usually grilled or cubed in a casserole.

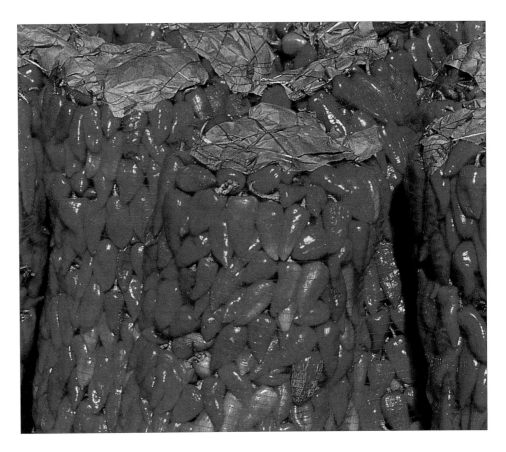

SOUPS

Many foreigners asked to nominate their favourite Balkan dish might elect bean soup. While all East European countries have their individual recipes for bean soup, it is the addition of hot and sour elements by Romanian and Bulgarian cooks that earns their soups a first prize for texture and sheer gutsy flavour. The distinctive sour tang is usually provided by lemon juice but can also be from vinegar, bitter fruits or pickles.

Tarator, an unusual cold soup made with cucumber, yogurt and walnuts, is a delicious example of some of the region's excellent and refreshing summer cooking.

DESSERTS

A sweet course in Romania might be a cherry strudel, a sweet jam- or fruit-filled pancake reminiscent of an Austrian favourite. The classic Bulgarian dessert, usually a creamy rice pudding, is flavoured with rose

Above: Sacks of fresh red chillies ready for sale in a Serbian market. Peppers are used both fresh and pickled.

water. In Slovenia it might be a rich, sweet, boiled pudding, almost Anglo-Saxon in style, such as *potica*, which may be made using buckwheat flour and chestnuts.

Chestnuts, walnuts and other nuts such as pistachios are widely used in sweet bakery. They make an appearance in French-inspired tarts as well as in Eastern-style cakes that drip syrup, as typified by *baklava*.

Any Balkan meal might end with a Turkish-style coffee, served with what the Romanians call a *dulceata* and the Serbians a *slatko*. These sweetmeats consist of either Turkish delight or soft sweets made from apples, plums, raisins, sultanas or figs, which have been stewed, thickened and rolled into balls, before perhaps being coated with nuts. They may be dipped in rum or other alcohol.

INGREDIENTS

Left, from front: tomatoes, capsicum, large fresh chillies, aubergines, courgettes, cucumber and beans.

Below, from the back: salmon, grey mullet, octopus, sea bass, mackerel, whitebait and trout.

VEGETABLES
Southern vegetables such as peppers, aubergines, courgettes and tomatoes all feature strongly in Balkan cuisine, together with more northerly onions and cabbage. Piquant stews of peppers and aubergines with garlic, vinegar and oil are used as relishes or cooked salads served with bread. Romanian grilled meat dishes are often accompanied by pickled vegetables, such as cucumbers or chillies.

FISH
The predominant inland fish, that might once have been caught in the Danube, are carp, grey mullet, river trout, sturgeon and sterlet, pike, perch, bream and freshwater crayfish. Traditionally, excellent catfish comes from the Danube delta, while on the Adriatic coast squid and octopus are caught, as well as mackerel, sardines, tuna and white fish such as sea bass and gilt-head bream. Species found in the Black Sea include grey mullet and scad, small oily fish which resemble whitebait and are fried in batter and eaten whole.

DAIRY PRODUCTS
Kashkaval, properly made from ewe's milk, is the general name for the yellow cheese produced in the Balkans. Depending on how it is made it can be piquant, or rubbery and bland. It is often available from Greek, Middle Eastern and Cypriot delicatessens and is excellent for grating, toasting and frying. A good substitute is Italian pecorino. *Brinza* is the Romanian equivalent of the brine cheese used throughout East European cooking, for which feta may be substituted.

Bulgarian yogurt has become a legendary source of health and longevity, but it may be replaced by any good quality live organic yogurt. It is the key ingredient in a cold cucumber soup of the region. A unique Serbian speciality is *kaimak*, which is thick cream made from boiled milk.

Far left, clockwise from left: red kidney beans, mamaliga, *haricot beans and black kidney beans.*

Left, clockwise from left: peaches, lemons, oranges, apricots, cherries, pistachios and shelled walnuts.

GRAINS AND PULSES

Mamaliga, cooked cornmeal used as a staple accompaniment to meat dishes, or with cheese or bacon, is a distinctive Romanian speciality, although it is now encountered less often than it was 50 years ago. The tradition of making this bright yellow porridge came to Europe from the New World in the 16th century, and it has remained a favourite also with the Italians, who call it polenta.

The handground cornmeal was cooked in water over an open fire until it was so thick that it could be sliced like bread when cool. The tools for making *mamaliga*, an iron cauldron and a large wooden stirring stick, are prized decorative objects.

Red and black kidney beans and white haricot or lima beans are widely used in soups.

FRUIT AND NUTS

Cherries, peaches, apricots, figs and watermelons are widely enjoyed when in season. Chestnuts form an important part of sweet baking in some regions such as Slovenia, as do apples, and Balkan pastries of all kinds are filled with the walnuts and hazelnuts that grow in abundance. Walnuts are also used to thicken the typical cold soups.

HERBS, SPICES AND OTHER FLAVOURINGS

Fresh herbs such as parsley, thyme, tarragon, basil, savory, mint and dill are widely used in the Balkans – in salads, soups and casseroles. Chilli peppers give a typical fire to Balkan cooking. A more unusual herb, lovage, comparable with the taste of celery leaves, is typically used in Romanian cooking, especially in lamb soup. It is not difficult to buy and is also easily grown at home. The Balkan countries also have a taste for soups soured with lemon juice or a dash of vinegar.

Rose water and rose petals flavour and decorate Bulgarian desserts, such as rice puddings. The Valley of the Roses, which crosses Bulgaria from west to east, was planted by the Turks in the 17th century; since then, it has become the home of the precious oil called rose attar, and the basis of a small industry in soap and rose liqueur.

Right, clockwise from front left: fresh chillies, vinegar, olive oil, fresh herbs, rose water and petals, dried thyme, Kashkaval *ewe's milk cheese, yogurt and olives (centre).*

DRINKS

Coffee of the strong, thick Turkish variety is widely loved throughout the Balkans and east Adriatic countries. It is often served with an accompanying sweetmeat such as *lokum* (Turkish delight).

Maraschino, made of cherries, *travarica*, flavoured with herbs, and *slivovica* (slivowicz), a plum brandy, are all popular liqueurs in the countries of the former Yugoslavia. The Romanian national spirit is *tuica*, a very potent plum eau de vie or brandy. Bulgaria produces a rose liqueur and also one of aniseed, called *mastica*, which is similar to the Greek raki.

SOUPS AND STARTERS

East Europeans are renowned for their hospitality, and home-made soup is often to be found on the stove, ready for eating at any time of the day. Sour-flavoured soups, called chorbas, are a traditional speciality of this region, as is the unusual combination of fruit and vegetables in their soups.

Meze, or starters, reflect the typical flavours and ingredients of the region, such as local cheeses, fresh fish and seafood, tomatoes, capsicums and herbs and spices. Served hot or cold, they are the perfect beginning to a meal.

Cold Cucumber and Yogurt Soup with Walnuts

A refreshing cold soup, using a classic combination of cucumber and yogurt, typical of the area.

INGREDIENTS

Serves 5–6
1 cucumber
4 garlic cloves
2.5ml/½ tsp salt
75g/3oz/¾ cup walnut pieces
40g/1½ oz day-old bread, torn into pieces
30ml/2 tbsp walnut or sunflower oil
400ml/14fl oz/1⅔ cups cow's or sheep's yogurt
120ml/4fl oz/½ cup cold water or chilled still mineral water
5–10ml/1–2 tsp lemon juice

For the garnish
40g/1½ oz/scant ½ cup walnuts, coarsely chopped
25ml/1½ tbsp olive oil
sprigs of fresh dill

1 Cut the cucumber into 2 and peel one half of it. Dice the cucumber flesh and set aside.

2 Using a large mortar and pestle, crush the garlic and salt together well; add the walnuts and bread.

— COOK'S TIP —

If you prefer your soup smooth, purée it in a food processor or blender before serving.

3 When the mixture is smooth, add the walnut or sunflower oil slowly and combine well.

4 Transfer the mixture into a large bowl and beat in the yogurt and diced cucumber.

5 Add the cold water or mineral water and lemon juice to taste.

6 Pour the soup into chilled soup bowls to serve. Garnish with the coarsely chopped walnuts, a little olive oil drizzled over the nuts and sprigs of fresh dill.

Bulgarian Sour Lamb Soup

This soup – a variation on the basic traditional sour soup, or *chorba* – has long been associated with Bulgaria. This recipe uses lamb, though pork or poultry are also popular.

INGREDIENTS

Serves 4–5
30ml/2 tbsp oil
450g/1lb lean lamb, trimmed
 and cubed
1 onion, diced
30ml/2 tbsp plain flour
15ml/1 tbsp paprika
1 litre/1³/₄ pints/4 cups hot lamb stock
3 parsley sprigs
4 spring onions
4 dill sprigs
25g/1oz/scant ¹/₄ cup long-grain rice
2 eggs, beaten
30–45ml/2–3 tbsp or more vinegar
 or lemon juice
salt and freshly ground black pepper
crusty bread, to serve

For the garnish
25g/1oz/2 tbsp butter, melted
5ml/1 tsp paprika
a little parsley or lovage and dill

1 In a large pan heat the oil and then brown the meat. Add the onion and cook until it has softened.

2 Sprinkle in the flour and paprika. Stir well, add the stock and cook for 10 minutes.

3 Tie the parsley, spring onions and dill together with string and add to the pan with the rice and a little salt and pepper. Bring to the boil then simmer for about 30–40 minutes, or until the lamb is tender.

--- COOK'S TIP ---

Do not reheat this soup since the eggs could become scrambled.

4 Remove the pan from the heat then add the beaten eggs, stirring continuously. Add the vinegar or lemon juice. Remove and discard the tied herbs and season to taste.

5 For the garnish, melt the butter and paprika together in a small pan. Ladle the soup into warmed serving bowls. Garnish with herbs and a little red paprika butter. Serve with thick chunks of bread.

Apple Soup

Romania has vast fruit orchards, and this soup is a delicious result of that natural resource.

INGREDIENTS

Serves 6
1 kohlrabi
3 carrots
2 celery sticks
1 green pepper, seeded
2 tomatoes
45ml/3 tbsp oil
2 litres/3½ pints/8 cups
   chicken stock
6 large green apples
45ml/3 tbsp plain flour
150ml/¼ pint/⅔ cup double cream
15ml/1 tbsp granulated sugar
30–45ml/2–3 tbsp lemon juice
salt and freshly ground black pepper
lemon wedges and crusty bread,
   to serve

1 Dice the kohlrabi, carrots, celery, green pepper and tomatoes in a large pan, add the oil and fry for 5–6 minutes until just softened.

2 Pour in the chicken stock, bring to the boil then reduce the heat and simmer for 45 minutes.

3 Meanwhile, peel, core and dice the apples, then add to the pan and simmer for a further 15 minutes.

4 In a bowl, mix together the flour and double cream then pour slowly into the soup, stirring well, and bring to the boil. Add the sugar and lemon juice before seasoning to taste. Serve immediately accompanied by lemon wedges and crusty bread.

Chick-pea Soup

Chick-peas form part of the staple diet in the Balkans, used either whole or ground. This soup is economical to make, and various spicy sausages may be added to give extra flavour.

INGREDIENTS

Serves 4–6
500g/1¼lb/3½ cups chick-peas,
   rinsed and drained well
2 litres/3½ pints/8 cups chicken or
   vegetable stock
3 large waxy potatoes, peeled and cut
   into bite-size chunks
50ml/2fl oz/¼ cup olive oil
225g/8oz spinach leaves, washed and
   drained well
salt and freshly ground black pepper

1 Place the chick-peas in a bowl of cold water and leave overnight. The next day, drain them well and place in a large pan with the stock.

2 Bring to the boil, then reduce the heat and cook gently for about 55 minutes. Add the potatoes, olive oil and seasoning, and cook for 20 minutes.

3 Five minutes before the end of cooking, add the spinach. Serve the soup in warmed soup bowls.

Lamb Meatball Soup with Vegetables

This family recipe is an ideal way to use up leftover vegetables.

INGREDIENTS

Serves 4
1 litre/1³/₄ pints/4 cups lamb stock
1 onion, finely chopped
2 carrots, finely sliced
¹/₂ celeriac, finely diced
75g/3oz/³/₄ cup frozen peas
50g/2oz green beans, cut into
   2.5cm/1in pieces
3 tomatoes, seeded and chopped
1 red pepper, seeded and finely diced
1 potato, coarsely diced
2 lemons, sliced
salt and freshly ground black pepper
crusty bread, to serve

For the meatballs
225g/8oz very lean minced lamb
40g/1¹/₂oz/¹/₄ cup short-grain rice
30ml/2 tbsp chopped fresh parsley
plain flour, for coating
salt and freshly ground black pepper

1 Put the stock, all of the vegetables, the slices of lemon and a little seasoning in a large pan. Bring to the boil, then reduce the heat and simmer for 15–20 minutes.

2 Meanwhile, for the meatballs, combine the minced meat, rice and parsley together in a bowl and season well.

3 Roll the mixture into small balls, roughly the size of walnuts and toss them in the flour.

4 Drop the meatballs into the soup and simmer gently for 25–30 minutes, stirring occasionally, to prevent the meatballs from sticking. Adjust the seasoning to taste and serve the soup in warmed serving bowls, accompanied by crusty bread.

Romanian Bean Soup

With Central Europe to the west and the former Yugoslavia and Turkey to the south and east, Romanian cuisine is a mix of hearty flavours, as proved by this soup with mixed beans, smoked pork, chilli and onion.

INGREDIENTS

Serves 6

450g/1lb/2½ cups dried mixed beans, thoroughly rinsed and drained
300g/11oz smoked pork, plus a ham bone
30ml/2 tbsp lard or vegetable oil
1 onion, sliced
1–2 fresh red chillies, seeded and diced
50g/2oz plain flour
20g/³⁄₄oz paprika
30ml/2 tbsp vinegar
salt and freshly ground black pepper
bread, to serve

1 Put the dried beans in a large bowl. Pour enough cold water to cover and leave to soak overnight. When ready to cook, drain and rinse the beans thoroughly.

COOK'S TIP

For a hearty main course meal, serve this soup poured over freshly cooked pasta, and topped with a little grated Parmesan.

2 Place the beans in a large pan and cover with water. Add the pork and ham bone, bring to the boil, reduce the heat and cover. Cook for 2–2½ hours.

3 In a frying pan, heat the lard or oil then cook the onion and chillies for 3–4 minutes or until pale golden. Remove from the heat, sprinkle in the flour and paprika and stir well.

4 Remove the meat and discard the bone. Cut the meat into even pieces and return to the pan. Stir in the onion mixture and the vinegar.

5 Bring the soup to the boil, stirring well. Season to taste. Serve with chunks of bread.

Bessarabian Pancakes

Bessarabia is the historical name for modern Moldova, in Romania, the source for this spinach and cheese pancake.

INGREDIENTS

Serves 4–6
4 eggs, beaten
40g/1½ oz/3tbsp butter, melted
250ml/8fl oz/1 cup single cream
250ml/8fl oz/1 cup soda water
175g/6oz/1½ cups plain flour, sifted
pinch of salt
1 egg white, lightly beaten
oil, for frying

For the filling
350g/12oz/1½ cups feta
  cheese, crumbled
50g/2oz/⅔ cup Parmesan
  cheese, grated
40g/1½oz/3 tbsp butter
1 garlic clove, crushed
450g/1lb frozen spinach, thawed
shavings of Parmesan, to garnish

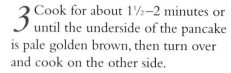

1 Blend the eggs, butter, cream and water in a food processor or blender. With the motor running, spoon in the flour and salt through the feeder tube until the batter mixture is smooth and lump free. Leave to stand for 15 minutes to rest, loosely covered with clear film.

2 Lightly grease a 13–15cm/5–6in non-stick frying pan and place over a medium heat. When hot, pour in 45–60ml/3–4 tbsp of the batter, tilting the pan to spread the mixture thinly.

3 Cook for about 1½–2 minutes or until the underside of the pancake is pale golden brown, then turn over and cook on the other side.

4 Repeat the process until all the batter has been used, stacking the pancakes on a warm plate as you go.

5 For the filling, in a clean bowl mix together well the crumbled feta and Parmesan cheese, the butter and garlic clove. Thoroughly stir in the squeeze-dried spinach.

6 Place 30–45ml/2–3 tbsp of the filling mixture on to the centre of each pancake. Brush a little egg white around the outer edges of the pancakes and then fold them over. Press the edges down well to seal.

7 Fry the pancakes in a little oil on both sides, turning gently, until they are golden brown and the filling is hot. Serve immediately, garnished with Parmesan shavings.

Fried Peppers with Cheese

This traditional Bulgarian dish may vary slightly from place to place in the Balkan area, but it is usually served as a starter or light snack. The peppers may be red, yellow or green.

INGREDIENTS

Serves 2–4

4 long peppers
50g/2oz/½ cup plain flour, seasoned
1 egg, beaten
olive oil, for shallow frying
cucumber and tomato salad,
    to serve

For the filling

1 egg, beaten
90g/3½ oz/scant ½ cup feta cheese,
    finely crumbled
30ml/2 tbsp chopped fresh parsley
1 small chilli, seeded and
    finely chopped

1 Slit open the peppers lengthways, enabling you to scoop out the seeds and remove the cores, but leaving the peppers in one piece.

2 Carefully open out the peppers and place under a preheated grill, skin side uppermost. Cook until the skin is charred and blackened. Place the peppers on a plate, cover with clear film and leave for 10 minutes.

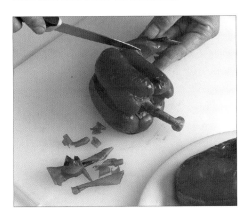

3 Using a sharp knife, carefully peel away the skin from the peppers.

4 In a bowl mix together well all the filling ingredients. Divide evenly among the four peppers.

5 Reshape the peppers to look whole. Dip them into the seasoned flour, then the egg then the flour again.

6 Fry the peppers gently in a little olive oil for 6–8 minutes, turning once, or until golden brown and the filling is set. Drain the peppers on kitchen paper before serving with a cucumber and tomato salad.

Stuffed Cabbage Rolls

Fresh cabbage is available all year round in large quantities and many households also use pickled versions in their cooking. Every cook will have a favourite version of this recipe.

INGREDIENTS

Makes 10–15

1 white cabbage, cored
200g/7oz/1 cup long-grain rice
75g/3oz/6 tbsp butter
1 onion, finely chopped
300g/11oz mixture of minced pork, veal and lamb
50g/2oz bacon, rinded and chopped
1 egg, beaten
15ml/1 tbsp chopped fresh flat leaf parsley
2 garlic cloves, crushed
75ml/5 tbsp water
thyme leaves, to garnish

For the tomato sauce

20g/³⁄₄oz/scant 2 tbsp butter
20g/³⁄₄oz/3 tbsp flour
397g/14oz can chopped plum tomatoes with garlic
120ml/4fl oz/¹⁄₂ cup chicken stock
sprig of fresh thyme
generous pinch of sugar
salt and freshly ground black pepper

1 Preheat the oven to 190°C/375°F/ Gas 5. Place the cabbage in a large pan of lightly salted water and cook for 30 minutes. Drain and leave to cool. Meanwhile, boil the rice until only just cooked.

2 Melt the butter and gently cook the onion for 2–3 minutes until soft but not browned. Add the meat and bacon and cook until browned; add the rice, egg, parsley and garlic.

3 Lay the cabbage leaves out and, if the rib is too thick, trim to remove. Divide the meat mixture among the leaves. Roll them up and place in a greased ovenproof dish.

4 Sprinkle over the water, cover and cook for 30 minutes in the oven.

5 Meanwhile, put all the sauce ingredients together in a pan and bring to the boil, stirring all the time. Reduce the heat to a simmer and cook for a further 20 minutes. Serve the stuffed cabbage leaves with the tomato sauce poured over them and sprinkled with thyme leaves.

Cheese Scrolls

These delicious Bulgarian cheese savouries are traditionally served warm as a first course, or else as a snack in cafés, restaurants and homes at any time of the day.

INGREDIENTS

Makes 14–16

450g/1lb/2 cups feta cheese, well
    drained and finely crumbled
90ml/6 tbsp natural Greek yogurt
2 eggs, beaten
14–16 sheets 40 × 30cm/16 × 12in
    ready-made filo pastry, thawed
    if frozen
225g/8oz/1 cup unsalted butter,
    melted
sea salt and chopped spring onions,
    to garnish

1 Preheat the oven to 200°C/400°F/ Gas 6. In a large bowl mix together the feta cheese, yogurt and eggs, beating well until the mixture is smooth.

2 Fit a piping bag with a large 1cm/ ½in plain round nozzle and fill with half of the cheese mixture.

COOK'S TIP

If possible, use the locally made sheep's cheese, *bryndza*. Made throughout Eastern Europe, it is a subtly flavoured, crumbly and moist cheese that resembles feta, but it is not as salty. It is increasingly available in Middle Eastern or Cypriot delicatessens.

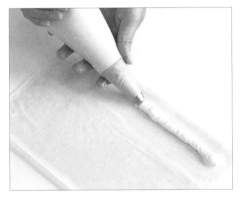

3 Lay out one sheet of pastry, fold into a 30 × 20cm/12 × 8in rectangle and brush with a little melted butter. Along one long edge pipe the cheese mixture 5mm/¼in away from the edge.

4 Roll up the pastry to form a sausage shape and tuck in each end, to prevent the filling escaping. Brush with more melted butter.

5 Form the "sausage" into a tight "S" or a crescent shape. Repeat with the remaining ingredients, refilling the piping bag as necessary.

6 Arrange the scrolls on a buttered baking sheet and sprinkle with a little sea salt and chopped spring onion. Bake for 20 minutes, or until golden brown and crispy. Cool on a wire rack, before serving.

Aubergine and Pepper Spread

This spread is typical of rich, cooked vegetable mixtures, which can be used on breads, as a dip or with grilled meat.

INGREDIENTS

Serves 6–8
675g/1½lb aubergines,
    halved lengthways
2 green peppers, seeded and quartered
45ml/3 tbsp olive oil
2 firm ripe tomatoes, halved, seeded
    and finely chopped
45ml/3 tbsp chopped fresh parsley
    or coriander
2 garlic cloves, crushed
30ml/2 tbsp red wine vinegar
lemon juice, to taste
salt and freshly ground black pepper
sprigs of parsley or coriander,
    to garnish
dark rye bread and lemon wedges,
    to serve

1 Place the aubergines and peppers under a preheated grill, skin side uppermost, and cook until the skin blisters and chars. Turn the vegetables over and cook for a further 3 minutes. Place in a polythene bag and leave for 10 minutes.

2 Peel away the blackened skin and purée the aubergine and pepper flesh in a food processor.

3 With the motor running, pour the olive oil in a continuous stream, through the feeder tube.

4 Carefully remove the blade and stir in the chopped tomatoes, parsley or coriander, garlic, vinegar and lemon juice. Season to taste, garnish with fresh parsley or coriander and serve with dark rye bread and wedges of lemon.

Tarama

This well-known hors d'oeuvre is made from hard fish roes, generally from grey mullet or cod, to which salt has been added as a preservative.

INGREDIENTS

Serves 4–6
115g/4oz/8 tbsp smoked tarama or
    cod's roe
15ml/1 tbsp lemon juice
175ml/6fl oz/¾ cup olive oil, plus a
    little extra for drizzling
20g/¾oz finely grated onion
15–25ml/1–1½ tbsp boiling water
paprika, for sprinkling
black olives and celery leaves,
    to garnish
toast, to serve

1 Soak the cod's roe in cold water for 2 hours. Drain, then peel off any outer skin and membrane from the roe and discard it. Process the roe in a food processor or blender at a low speed.

2 Add the lemon juice and then, with the motor still running, slowly add the olive oil through the feeder tube.

3 Once thickened, beat in the onion and water. Spoon into a serving bowl and chill well. Sprinkle with a little paprika. Garnish with the olives and celery leaves. Drizzle with a little oil and serve with toasted bread.

Grilled Pepper Salad

This Romanian dish, *Salata de Ardei*, is generally served as a starter (*meze*), or as a dish to accompany cold meats. *Meze* are served on a flat dish divided into different sections so that another three or four complementary *meze* may be added, such as diced salami, feta cheese, olives or pickle.

INGREDIENTS

Serves 4

8 long green and/or orange peppers
1 garlic clove, crushed
75ml/5 tbsp olive oil
60ml/4 tbsp wine vinegar
4 tomatoes, sliced
1 red onion, thinly sliced
freshly ground black pepper
sprigs of fresh coriander,
    to garnish
black bread, to serve

1 Cut the peppers into quarters, discarding the cores, seeds and tops. Place under a preheated grill, skin side uppermost, and cook until the skin chars and blisters.

--- COOK'S TIP ---

The long peppers used in this recipe are increasingly available, but if you cannot find them use small ordinary peppers.

2 Place the peppers in a polythene bag and leave for 15 minutes.

3 Remove the peppers from the bag and scrape off the skins using a sharp knife.

4 Blend together the garlic, olive oil and vinegar. Arrange the peppers, tomatoes and onion on four serving plates and pour over the garlic dressing. Season, garnish with sprigs of coriander and serve with black bread.

Octopus Salad

The Adriatic Sea separates Italy and the former Yugoslavian countries, which accounts for many of the similarities between their cuisines – particularly in their fondness for fresh fish and seafood, olives, oil and vinegar.

INGREDIENTS

Serves 4–6

900g/2lb baby octopus or squid, skinned
175ml/6fl oz/³/₄ cup olive oil
30ml/2 tbsp white wine vinegar
30ml/2 tbsp chopped fresh parsley or coriander
12 black olives, stoned
2 shallots, thinly sliced
1 red onion, thinly sliced
salt and freshly ground black pepper
sprigs of coriander, to garnish
8–12 cos lettuce leaves and lemon wedges, to serve

1 In a large saucepan, boil the octopus or squid in salted water for 20–25 minutes, or until just soft. Strain and leave to cool before covering and chilling for 45 minutes.

COOK'S TIP

Take care not to overcook the octopus or squid or it will become tough and rubbery.

2 Cut the tentacles from the body and head, then chop all the flesh into even pieces, slicing across the thick part of the tentacles following the direction of the suckers.

3 In a bowl, combine the olive oil and white wine vinegar.

4 Add the parsley, olives, shallots, octopus and red onion to the bowl. Season to taste and toss well.

5 Arrange the octopus on a bed of lettuce, garnish with coriander and serve with lemon wedges.

Poached Eggs with Yogurt

In this Bulgarian recipe, the combination of yogurt and garlic to make a sauce is typical of the region, and is a surprisingly tasty accompaniment to freshly cooked poached eggs.

INGREDIENTS

Serves 4

2 garlic cloves
225g/8oz/1 cup thick natural
   set yogurt
4–8 eggs (1–2 per person, to taste)
30ml/2 tbsp vinegar
salt
freshly cooked spinach and crusty
   bread, to serve

For the paprika butter

50g/2oz/4 tbsp butter
15ml/1 tbsp paprika or chilli powder,
   plus extra for sprinkling

1 Using a pestle and mortar, grind the garlic with a pinch of salt to a paste. Stir the garlic into the yogurt then divide between serving bowls.

2 Gently break the eggs into a pan of boiling water with the vinegar added. Cover the pan and lower the heat. Cook the eggs for 2–3 minutes, or until set to your preference. Remove with a slotted spoon to drain well.

3 Place 1–2 eggs in each bowl and season with salt. Melt the butter in a small pan with the paprika or chilli.

4 Strain the paprika butter evenly over the eggs and yogurt. Serve hot with spinach and bread and sprinkle with paprika or chilli powder.

Deep-fried Cheese

This tasty Bulgarian appetizer is traditionally made with *kashkaval* cheese, but the Italian provolone is a good substitute, as is any good melting cheese such as haloumi or fontina. Serve immediately once cooked.

INGREDIENTS

Serves 5–6

450g/1lb kashkaval or provolone
plain flour, for coating
2–3 eggs, beaten
115–175g/4–6oz/2–3 cups fresh
   breadcrumbs or fine matzo meal
oil for deep frying
lovage or flat leaf parsley, to garnish

1 Cut the cheese into 1cm/½in thick even slices. Tip the flour, beaten egg and breadcrumbs or matzo meal on to separate plates, ready for coating.

2 Dip the cheese slices into the flour, then into the egg and finally into the breadcrumbs or matzo. Shake off any residual crumbs.

3 Heat the oil to 180°C/350°F in a deep pan and fry the cheese in batches. Drain on kitchen paper and keep warm until all the cheese slices are cooked. Garnish with some sprigs of lovage or flat leaf parsley.

MEAT AND POULTRY

Lamb has long reigned supreme throughout the Balkans, and it has resulted in many delicious dishes, such as the classic kebab and slowly cooked casseroles and stews, and pastry-encased whole joints for special occasions.

Balkan cooking has been shaped by many influences, producing a surprising variety. The recipe for Pork Schnitzel, combining soured cream with pork, is reminiscent of its northern neighbours Hungary and Austria, and the addition of spices to Rolled Beef gives that dish a distinctive Turkish flavour.

Lamb-stuffed Squash

This recipe is ideal for using any leftover cooked meat and rice.

INGREDIENTS

Serves 6 as a main course, 12 as a starter
6 acorn squash, halved
45ml/3tbsp lemon juice
25g/1oz/2 tbsp butter
30ml/2 tbsp plain flour
250ml/8fl oz/1 cup whipping cream
175ml/6fl oz/³/₄ cup passata
115g/4oz/½ cup feta cheese, crumbled
    and basil leaves, to garnish, plus
    extra, to serve

For the filling
350–450g/12–16oz cooked lean lamb
175g/6oz cooked long-grain rice
25g/1oz/2 tbsp butter, melted
25g/1oz/½ cup fresh breadcrumbs
50ml/2fl oz/¹/₄ cup milk
30ml/2 tbsp finely grated onion
30ml/2 tbsp chopped fresh parsley
2 eggs, beaten
salt and freshly ground black pepper

1 Preheat the oven to 180°C/350°F/ Gas 4. Trim the bases of the squash, if necessary, so that they will stand up securely. Using a teaspoon, remove the insides of the squash, taking care not to cut the outer skin or base. Leave about 1cm/½in of flesh from the base.

2 Blanch the squash in boiling water with the lemon juice for 2–3 minutes, then plunge them into cold water. Drain well and leave to cool.

3 Meanwhile, make the filling by combining in a bowl the cooked lamb and rice, the butter, breadcrumbs, milk, onion, parsley, eggs and seasoning. Place the squash in a lightly greased ovenproof dish, and fill with the lamb mixture.

4 To make the sauce, put the butter and flour in a pan. Whisk in the cream and bring to the boil, whisking all the time. Cook for 1–2 minutes until thickened, then season well. Pour the sauce over the prepared squash, then pour over the passata.

5 Bake the squash in the oven for 25–30 minutes. Drizzle them with a little of the sauce, and sprinkle with feta cheese and basil leaves. Serve separately any extra sauce, feta and basil.

COOK'S TIP

You could use a thick courgette or a marrow instead of the squash, removing the seeds in the same way.

Bulgarian Lamb in Pastry

This is an impressive dish to serve on special occasions. Skim the meat juices, bring them back to the boil and serve as a gravy with the lamb.

INGREDIENTS

Serves 6–8

1.5kg/3½ lb leg of lamb, boned
40g/1½ oz/3 tbsp butter
2.5ml/½ tsp each dried thyme, basil
  and oregano
2 garlic cloves, crushed
45ml/3tbsp lemon juice
salt, for sprinkling
1 egg, beaten, for sealing and glazing
1 oregano or marjoram sprig,
  to garnish

For the pastry

450g/1lb/4 cups plain flour, sifted
250g/9oz/generous 1 cup chilled
  butter, diced
150–250ml/¼–½ pint/²⁄₃–1 cup
  iced water

1 Preheat the oven to 190°/375°F/ Gas 5. To make the pastry, place the flour and butter into a food processor or blender and process until the mixture resembles fine breadcrumbs. Add enough iced water to make a soft, but not sticky, dough. Knead gently and form into a ball. Wrap in clear film and refrigerate for 1–2 hours.

2 Meanwhile, put the lamb in a roasting tin, tie the joint with string and cut 20 small holes in the meat, with a sharp, narrow knife.

3 Cream together the butter, dried herbs, garlic and lemon juice and use to fill the small cuts in the lamb. Sprinkle the whole joint with salt.

4 Cook the lamb in a roasting tin for about 1 hour, then allow to cool. Remove the string.

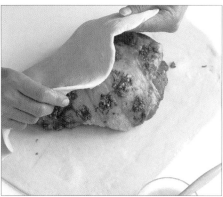

5 Roll out the pastry on a lightly floured surface until large enough to wrap around the lamb in one piece. Seal the pastry edges with a little of the egg and place in a clean tin.

6 With any remaining scraps of pastry make leaves or other shapes to decorate the pastry. Brush with more of the egg. Return to the oven and bake for a further 30–45 minutes. Serve hot, in slices, accompanied by the gravy from the meat juices, and garnished with a sprig of oregano or marjoram.

Baked Lamb with Potatoes Under a Bell

Traditionally this recipe was prepared in a metal dish of two parts: a round base and a domed top, shaped like a bell, and was then cooked in a fireplace called a *komin*.

INGREDIENTS

Serves 10–16
about 1.5–1.75kg/3–4lb, knuckle of
   lamb or half shoulder
900g/2lb firm potatoes, such as
   Cypress, thickly sliced
2 onions, roughly chopped
handful of fresh parsley and rosemary
   plus extra to garnish
salt and freshly ground black pepper
country-style bread and an okra,
   pepper and haricot or cannellini
   bean salad, to serve

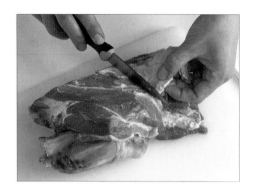

1 Preheat the oven to 150°C/300°F/ Gas 2. Trim off any excess fat from the lamb. Place the lamb in a very heavy metal casserole pot with a tight-fitting lid.

—————— COOK'S TIP ——————

If using a barbecue, sit the metal casserole on a brick and ensure the coals are very hot. Add more coals as necessary.

2 Arrange the potatoes and onion around the lamb.

3 Scatter the fresh herbs around the meat. Season very well and cover.

4 Cook the lamb for 4–5 hours, or until the meat and potatoes are golden brown and very tender. Garnish with more fresh herbs and serve with country bread and a salad of okra, peppers and beans.

Romanian Chilli

This spicy dish is a tasty amalgam of a number of influences – Italian and Turkish.

INGREDIENTS

Serves 4–6
30ml/2 tbsp oil
1 onion, finely chopped
2 green peppers, seeded and diced
15–30ml/1–2 tbsp chilli powder
675g/1½lb lean minced beef
300ml/½ pint/1¼ cups tomato sauce
   or passata
2 garlic cloves, crushed
2.5ml/½ tsp dried marjoram
2.5ml/½ tsp dried sage
397g/14oz can red kidney
   beans, drained
salt and freshly ground black pepper
whole and/or chopped chillies, to
   garnish (optional)
freshly cooked rice, to serve

1 Heat the oil in a frying pan and cook the onion for 1–1½ minutes, or until just beginning to soften.

2 Stir in the peppers and cook for a further 2–3 minutes.

3 Add the chilli powder and minced beef. Stir constantly until the meat browns. Add the tomato sauce and remaining ingredients, season well, then bring to the boil, stirring well.

4 Simmer for 10–15 minutes. Garnish with chillies if liked, and serve on a bed of rice.

Meat Loaf

Like many Serbian recipes, this dish is easy to make, requiring nothing more than good quality meat and plenty of fresh herbs.

INGREDIENTS

Serves 4–6
8 smoked streaky, rindless
   bacon rashers
2 lean bacon rashers, diced
1 onion, finely chopped
2 garlic cloves, crushed
115g/4oz/2 cups fresh breadcrumbs
90ml/6 tbsp milk
450g/1lb lean minced beef
450g/1lb lean minced pork
2.5ml/¹⁄₂ tsp chopped fresh thyme
30ml/2 tbsp chopped fresh parsley
2 eggs, beaten
salt and freshly ground black pepper
herby mashed potatoes and carrots,
   to serve

1 Preheat the oven to 200°C/400°F/Gas 6. Line a 1.75 litre/3 pint/7¹⁄₂ cup buttered loaf tin with the rashers of streaky bacon. Stretch the rashers with the back of a knife, if necessary, to completely fill the tin.

2 Dry fry the diced bacon in a large frying pan until almost crisp. Stir in the onion and garlic and fry for a further 2–3 minutes until they are soft and a pale golden brown.

3 In a large bowl soak the breadcrumbs in the milk for 5 minutes, or until all the milk is absorbed.

4 Add the minced meats, bacon, onion, garlic, herbs and eggs to the breadcrumbs. Season and mix well.

5 Spoon the mixture into the loaf tin. Level the top and cover the tin with foil. Bake for about 1¹⁄₂ hours. Turn out and serve in slices, with herby mashed potatoes and carrots.

Pork with Sauerkraut

The presence of sauerkraut and mustard suggests links with Central European cuisines, but the presence of chillies is a purely southern touch.

INGREDIENTS

Serves 4
450g/1lb lean pork or veal, diced
60ml/4 tbsp vegetable oil or
   melted lard
2.5ml/¹⁄₂ tsp paprika
400g/14oz shredded sauerkraut,
   drained and well rinsed
2 fresh red chillies
90ml/6 tbsp pork stock
salt and freshly ground black pepper
50ml/2fl oz/¹⁄₄ cup soured cream
coarse grain mustard, paprika and sage
   leaves, to garnish
crusty bread, to serve

1 In a heavy-based frying pan cook the pork or veal in the oil until browned on all sides.

2 Add the paprika and shredded sauerkraut. Stir well and transfer to a flameproof casserole.

3 Halve the chillies and remove the seeds before burying the chillies in the middle of the casserole.

4 Add the stock to the casserole. Cover tightly and cook over a gentle heat for 1–1¹⁄₂ hours, stirring occasionally to prevent it sticking.

5 Remove the chillies, if liked, and season to taste before serving. Spoon on the soured cream and spoonfuls of mustard, sprinkle with paprika and garnish with sage leaves. Serve with crusty bread.

Pork Schnitzel

This Croatian recipe features
Central European ingredients.

INGREDIENTS

Serves 4

4 pork leg steaks or escalopes, about
   200g/7oz each
60ml/4 tbsp olive oil
115g/4oz chicken livers, chopped
1 garlic clove, crushed
plain flour, seasoned, for coating
salt and freshly ground black pepper
15ml/1 tbsp chopped fresh parsley
   to garnish

For the sauce

1 onion, thinly sliced
115g/4oz streaky bacon, thinly sliced
175g/6oz/ 2 cups mixed wild
   mushrooms, sliced
120ml/4fl oz/½ cup olive oil
5ml/1 tsp ready-made mustard
150ml/¼ pint/⅔ cup white wine
120ml/4fl oz/½ cup soured cream
250ml/8fl oz/1 cup double cream
salt and freshly ground black pepper

1 Place the pork between 2 sheets of
dampened polythene, clear film or
greaseproof paper and flatten with a
meat mallet or rolling pin until about
15 × 10cm/6 × 4in. Season well.

2 Heat half the oil in a frying pan
and cook the chicken livers and
garlic for 1–2 minutes. Remove, drain
on kitchen paper and leave to cool.

--- COOK'S TIP ---

If liked, replace the pork with veal or
chicken and cook in the same way.

3 Divide the livers evenly between
the four prepared pork steaks and
roll up into neat parcels. Secure with
cocktail sticks or string before rolling
lightly in the seasoned flour.

4 Heat the remaining oil and gently
fry the schnitzels for 6–8 minutes
on each side, or until golden brown.
Drain on kitchen paper and keep warm.

5 Meanwhile, to make the sauce, fry
the onion, bacon and mushrooms
in the oil for 2–3 minutes, then add the
mustard, white wine and soured cream.
Stir to simmering point, then add the
double cream and season.

6 Arrange the schnitzels on plates
with a little of the sauce spooned
around and the rest poured into a
serving jug. Garnish with the parsley.

Spicy Rolled Beef

This recipe is a blend of Slovakian, Greek and Russian cuisines, with a spicy touch of coriander and peppercorns.

INGREDIENTS

Serves 4
4 thick 10–15cm/4–6in beef slices
50ml/2fl oz/¼ cup olive or vegetable oil, plus extra for frying
30ml/2 tbsp black peppercorns, roughly crushed
30ml/2 tbsp whole coriander seeds
1 onion, finely sliced
300ml/½ pint/1¼ cups Bulgarian or dry red wine
1 egg, beaten
150g/5oz can chopped tomatoes
polenta and soured cream, to serve

For the filling
115g/4oz/½ cup minced ham
40g/1½oz/scant 1 cup breadcrumbs
2 spring onions, finely sliced
45ml/3 tbsp chopped fresh parsley
1 egg yolk
75g/3oz green pepper, seeded and finely chopped
1.5ml/¼ tsp ground allspice

1 Place the slices of beef between 2 sheets of dampened polythene, clear film or greaseproof paper. Flatten with a meat mallet or rolling pin until the meat is evenly thin. Dip the slices in the oil.

2 Lay the meat out flat and sprinkle over the crushed peppercorns, coriander seeds and onion.

3 Roll up the meat neatly and place in a shallow glass or china dish. Pour over half of the wine, cover with clear film and chill for 2 hours.

4 Meanwhile, combine all the filling ingredients together in a bowl and add a little water or beef stock if necessary, to moisten the stuffing.

5 Remove the beef from the bowl and shake off the spices and onion. Spoon 30–45ml/2–3 tbsp of the filling into the middle of each piece of meat.

6 Brush the inner surface with egg and roll up well. Secure with a cocktail stick or tie with string.

7 Heat a little oil in a frying pan and sauté the rolls until brown on all sides. Reduce the heat and pour over the remaining wine and canned tomatoes. Simmer for 25–30 minutes, or until the meat is tender. Season well and serve the beef with the sauce, the polenta and soured cream and plenty of cracked pepper. Garnish with a sprig of parsley.

Charcoal-grilled Sausages

These little skinless sausages, *Mititei*, are made from minced beef and herbs and are found throughout Romania – eat them on their own as a snack or with rice and salad for a more substantial meal.

INGREDIENTS

Serves 6
900g/2lb lean minced beef
50g/2oz/scant ½ cup beef suet
3.5ml/¾ tsp ground cumin
2.5ml/½ tsp freshly ground
   black pepper
1 garlic clove, crushed
5ml/1 tsp salt
1.5ml/¼ tsp dried thyme
30ml/2 tbsp beef stock
tomato and spring onion salad and
   soured cream, to serve
paprika, for sprinkling

1 In a bowl, mix the beef, suet, cumin, pepper, garlic, salt, dried thyme and stock well together.

2 Divide the beef mixture into 18 equal portions.

— COOK'S TIP —

For extra spicy sausages add 2.5ml/½ tsp cayenne to the mixture before shaping.

3 With lightly floured hands, roll the portions into even oblongs.

4 Thread the sausages on skewers, if liked, and cook either on a barbecue or under a preheated grill.

5 Cook the sausages for 5–10 minutes or until cooked to your preference, turning them once during cooking. Serve immediately with a tomato and spring onion salad and soured cream, sprinkled with paprika.

Meatball Shish Kebab

The mix of aromatic herbs and spices gives these kebabs a wonderful flavour, which contrasts well with the boldness of the cabbage and dill pickles.

INGREDIENTS

Serves 4–6
800g/1¾lb lean lamb, diced
50g/2oz crustless white bread
1 onion, roughly chopped
5ml/1 tsp ground coriander
15ml/1 tbsp chopped fresh parsley
2.5ml/½ tsp ground cumin
2.5ml/½ tsp salt
oil, for basting
lemon wedges, stir-fried red cabbage
   and courgettes, plus dill pickles,
   to serve (optional)

1 Mince the lamb, bread and onion together, in a mincer, preferably, or put into a food processor, unclogging the blade when necessary.

2 Add the ground coriander, parsley, cumin and salt and mix well. With lightly dampened hands, shape the mixture into 32–36 even-size balls.

3 Gently, thread the meatballs on to 4–6 skewers.

4 Brush the kebabs with oil. Cook on a barbecue or under a preheated grill for 8–10 minutes, turning once during cooking. Baste occasionally to prevent drying out during cooking. Serve hot accompanied by lemon wedges, stir-fried red cabbage and courgettes and dill pickles, if liked.

Veal Escalopes

This simple dish is based on a German recipe, with the noodles adding a touch of the Mediterranean.

INGREDIENTS

Serves 4
4 veal escalopes, about 175g/6oz each
75g/3oz/²⁄₃ cup plain flour, seasoned
2 eggs, beaten
115g/4oz/scant 2 cups dried
    breadcrumbs
30ml/2 tbsp oil
50g/2oz/4 tbsp butter
coarsely ground white pepper
vegetable oil, for brushing
chives and paprika, to garnish
lemon wedges, buttered tagliatelle and
    green salad, to serve

1 Place the veal escalopes in between 2 sheets of dampened polythene, clear film or greaseproof paper and flatten with a meat mallet or rolling pin until half as large again. Press a little ground white pepper into both sides of the escalopes.

2 Tip the flour, eggs and breadcrumbs on to separate plates. Brush the meat with a little oil then dip into the flour. Shake off any extra flour. Then dip the escalopes into the egg and then finally the breadcrumbs. Leave, loosely covered, for 30 minutes.

3 Heat the oil and half of the butter together in a large frying pan and gently fry the escalopes, one at a time, over a gentle to medium heat for 3–4 minutes on each side. Be aware that too much heat will cause the veal to toughen. Keep the escalopes warm while you cook the remainder.

4 Top each escalope with one-quarter of the remaining butter. Garnish with chives and a sprinkling of paprika. Serve with lemon wedges and buttered tagliatelle, with a green salad or vegetable, if you like.

COOK'S TIP

To prevent the breadcrumb coating from cracking during cooking, use the back of a knife and lightly form a criss-cross pattern.

Romanian Kebab

Kebabs are popular world-wide, in great part because they are so easily adapted to suit everyone's taste. In this modern version, lean lamb is marinated then grilled with chunks of vegetables to produce a delicious, colourful and healthy meal. Traditionally, an unfermented grape juice (*mustarii*) and local bread is served with the meal.

INGREDIENTS

Serves 6
675g/1½lb lean lamb, cut into
    4cm/1½in cubes
12 shallots or button onions
2 green peppers, seeded and cut into
    12 pieces
12 small tomatoes
12 small mushrooms
sprigs of rosemary, to garnish
lemon slices, freshly cooked rice and
    crusty bread, to serve

For the marinade
juice of 1 lemon
120ml/4fl oz/½ cup red wine
1 onion, finely chopped
60ml/4 tbsp olive oil
2.5ml/½ tsp each dried sage
    and rosemary
salt and freshly ground black pepper

1 For the marinade, combine the lemon juice, red wine, onion, olive oil, herbs and seasoning in a bowl.

2 Stir the cubes of lamb into the marinade. Cover and refrigerate for 2–12 hours, stirring occasionally.

3 Remove the lamb from the marinade and thread the pieces on to 6 skewers alternating with the onions, peppers, tomatoes and mushrooms.

COOK'S TIP

To vary this recipe sprinkle over 30ml/ 2 tbsp chopped fresh parsley and finely chopped onion, to garnish.

4 Cook the kebabs over the hot coals of a barbecue or under a preheated grill for 10–15 minutes, turning them once. Use the leftover marinade to brush over the kebabs during cooking to prevent the meat drying out.

5 Serve the kebabs on a bed of freshly cooked rice, sprinkled with fresh rosemary and accompanied by lemon slices and slices of crusty bread.

Chicken with Beans

This substantial Bulgarian casserole is bursting with flavour, texture and colour.

INGREDIENTS

Serves 4–6
275g/10oz dried kidney or other
  beans, soaked overnight
8–12 chicken portions, such as thighs
  and drumsticks
12 bacon rashers, rinded
2 large onions, thinly sliced
250ml/8fl oz/1 cup dry white wine
2.5ml/½ tsp chopped fresh sage
  or oregano
2.5ml/½ tsp chopped fresh rosemary
generous pinch of nutmeg
150ml/¼ pint/⅔ cup soured cream
15ml/1 tbsp chilli powder or paprika
salt and freshly ground black pepper
sprigs of rosemary, to garnish
lemon wedges, to serve

1 Preheat the oven to 180°C/350°F/ Gas 4. Cook the beans in fast-boiling water for 20 minutes. Rinse and drain the beans well and trim the chicken pieces. Season the chicken with salt and pepper.

2 Arrange the bacon around the sides and base of an ovenproof dish. Sprinkle over half of the onion and then half the beans, followed by another layer of onion and then the remaining beans.

3 In a bowl combine the wine with half the fresh sage or oregano, rosemary and nutmeg. Pour over the onion and beans. In another bowl mix together the soured cream and the chilli powder or paprika.

4 Toss the chicken in the soured cream mixture and place on top of the beans. Cover with foil and bake for 1¼–1½ hours, removing the foil for the last 15 minutes of cooking. Serve garnished with rosemary and lemon.

Potted Chicken

This is a traditional Bulgarian way of cooking chicken – in a flameproof pot, on top of the stove – so that it cooks slowly and evenly in its own juices.

INGREDIENTS

Serves 6–8
8 chicken portions
6–8 firm ripe tomatoes, chopped
2 garlic cloves, crushed
3 onions, chopped
60ml/4 tbsp oil or melted lard
250ml/8fl oz/1 cup good chicken stock
2 bay leaves
10ml/2 tsp paprika
10 white peppercorns, bruised
handful of parsley, stalks reserved and
  leaves finely chopped
salt

1 Put the chicken, tomatoes and garlic in the flameproof pot. Cover and cook gently for 10–15 minutes.

----- COOK'S TIP -----

For extra flavour add 1 finely seeded chopped chilli pepper at Step 2.

2 Add the remaining ingredients, except the parsley leaves. Stir well.

3 Cover tightly and cook over a very low heat, stirring occasionally, for about 1¾–2 hours, or until the chicken is tender. Five minutes before the end of cooking, stir in the finely chopped parsley leaves.

Varna-style Chicken

In this tasty dish, the chicken is smothered in a rich, herby sauce.

INGREDIENTS

Serves 8
1.75kg/4lb chicken, cut into 8 pieces
2.5ml/¹⁄₂ tsp chopped fresh thyme
40g/1¹⁄₂oz/3 tbsp butter
45ml/3 tbsp vegetable oil
3–4 garlic cloves, crushed
2 onions, finely chopped
salt and freshly ground white pepper
basil and thyme leaves, to garnish
freshly cooked rice, to serve

For the sauce
120ml/4fl oz/¹⁄₂ cup dry sherry
45ml/3 tbsp tomato purée
a few fresh basil leaves
30ml/2 tbsp white wine vinegar
generous pinch of granulated sugar
5ml/1 tsp mild mustard
397g/14oz can chopped tomatoes
225g/8oz/3 cups mushrooms, sliced

1 Preheat the oven to 180°C/350°F/ Gas 4. Season the chicken with salt, pepper and thyme. In a large frying pan cook the chicken in the butter and oil, until golden brown. Remove from the frying pan, place in an ovenproof dish and keep hot.

--- COOK'S TIP ---

Replace the cultivated mushrooms with wild mushrooms, if liked, but do make sure they are cleaned thoroughly before using.

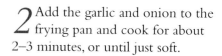

2 Add the garlic and onion to the frying pan and cook for about 2–3 minutes, or until just soft.

3 For the sauce, mix together the sherry, tomato purée, salt and pepper, basil, vinegar and sugar. Add the mustard and tomatoes. Pour into the frying pan and bring to the boil.

4 Reduce the heat and add the mushrooms. Adjust the seasoning with more sugar or vinegar to taste.

5 Pour the tomato sauce over the chicken. Bake in the oven, covered, for 45–60 minutes, or until cooked thoroughly. Serve on a bed of rice, garnished with basil and thyme.

Chicken Ghiveci

Romanians traditionally use a great variety of colourful seasonal vegetables in this hearty stew. A selection of home-grown herbs such as rosemary, marjoram and thyme, would also be added to flavour the stew.

INGREDIENTS

Serves 6

60ml/4 tbsp vegetable oil or
   melted lard
1 mild onion, thinly sliced
2 garlic cloves, crushed
2 red peppers, seeded and sliced
about 1.5kg/3½lb chicken
90ml/6 tbsp tomato purée
3 potatoes, diced
5ml/1 tsp chopped fresh rosemary
5ml/1 tsp chopped fresh marjoram
5ml/1 tsp chopped fresh thyme
3 carrots, cut into chunks
½ small celeriac, cut into chunks
120ml/4fl oz/½ cup dry white wine
2 courgettes, sliced
salt and freshly ground black pepper
chopped fresh rosemary and
   marjoram, to garnish
dark rye bread, to serve

1 Heat the oil in a large flameproof casserole. Add the onion and garlic and cook for 1–2 minutes until soft; then add the red peppers.

2 Joint the chicken into 6 pieces, place in the casserole and brown gently on all sides.

3 After about 15 minutes add the tomato purée, potatoes, herbs, carrots, celeriac and white wine, and season to taste with salt and pepper. Cook over a gentle heat, covered, for a further 40–50 minutes.

4 Add the courgette slices 5 minutes before the end of cooking. Adjust the seasoning to taste. Garnish with the herbs and serve with dark rye bread.

COOK'S TIP

If fresh herbs are unavailable, replace them with 2.5ml/½ tsp dried herbs.

Duckling Jubilee

This classic dish tastes delicious, and is very easily prepared.

INGREDIENTS

Serves 4
1.75kg/4½lb duckling
60ml/4 tbsp chopped fresh parsley
1 lemon, quartered
3 carrots, sliced
2 celery sticks, sliced
1 onion, roughly chopped
salt and freshly ground black pepper
apricots and sage flowers, to garnish

For the sauce
425g/15oz can apricots in syrup
50g/2oz/¼ cup granulated sugar
10ml/2 tsp English mustard
60ml/4 tbsp apricot jam
15ml/1 tbsp lemon juice
10ml/2 tsp freshly grated lemon rind
50ml/2fl oz/¼ cup fresh orange juice
1.5ml/¼ tsp each ginger and coriander
60–75ml/4–5 tbsp brandy

1 Preheat the oven to 220°C/425°F/Gas 7. Clean the duck well and pat dry with kitchen paper. Season the skin liberally.

2 Mix together the chopped parsley, lemon, carrots, celery sticks and onion in a bowl, then carefully spoon this into the cavity of the duck.

3 Cook the duck for 45 minutes on a trivet set over a roasting tin. Baste the duck occasionally with its juices.

4 Remove the duck from the oven and prick the skin well. Return it to the oven, reduce the temperature to 180°C/350°F/Gas 4, and cook for a further 1–1½ hours or until the duck is golden brown, tender and crispy.

5 Meanwhile, put the apricots and their syrup, the sugar and mustard in a food processor or blender. Add the jam and process until smooth.

6 Pour the apricot mixture into a pan and stir in the lemon juice and rind, orange juice and spices. Bring to the boil, add the brandy and cook for a further 1–2 minutes. Remove from the heat and adjust the seasoning.

7 Discard the fruit, vegetables and herbs from inside the duck and arrange the bird on a serving platter. Garnish with fresh apricots and sage flowers. Serve the sauce separately.

COOK'S TIP

If using a frozen duck, make sure it is thoroughly thawed before cooking.

Turkey Zador with Mlinces

A Croatian recipe for special occasion, the unusual *mlinces*, are used to soak up the juices.

INGREDIENTS

Serves 10–12
about 3kg/7lb turkey, well thawed
  if frozen
2 garlic cloves, halved
115g/4oz smoked bacon,
  finely chopped
30ml/2 tbsp chopped fresh rosemary
120ml/4fl oz/¹⁄₂ cup olive oil
250ml/8fl oz/1 cup dry white wine
grilled bacon, to serve
sprigs of rosemary, to garnish

For the *mlinces*
350g/12oz/3 cups plain flour, sifted
120–150ml/4–5fl oz/¹⁄₂–²⁄₃ cup
  warm water
30ml/2 tbsp oil
sea salt

1 Preheat the oven to 200°C/400°F/ Gas 6. Dry the turkey well inside and out using kitchen paper. Rub all over with the halved garlic.

2 Toss the bacon and rosemary together and use to stuff the turkey neck flap. Secure the skin underneath with a cocktail stick. Brush with the oil.

3 Place the turkey in a roasting tin and cover loosely with foil. Cook for 45–50 minutes. Remove the foil and reduce the oven temperature to 160°C/325°F/Gas 3.

4 Baste the turkey with the juices then pour over the white wine. Cook for 1 hour, basting occasionally with the juices. Reduce the temperature to 150°C/300°F/Gas 2, and continue to cook for a further 45 minutes, basting the turkey well.

5 Meanwhile, make the *mlinces* by kneading the flour with a little salt, the water and oil to make a soft but pliable dough. Divide equally into 4.

6 Roll out the dough thinly on a lightly floured surface into 40cm/ 16in circles. Sprinkle with salt. Bake on baking sheets alongside the turkey for 25 minutes until crisp. Crush into pieces about 6–10cm/2¹⁄₂–4in.

7 About 6–8 minutes before the end of the cooking time for the turkey add the *mlinces* to the meat juices alongside the turkey. Serve with grilled bacon, garnished with rosemary.

FISH

The numerous rivers, and the Adriatic and Black Seas that border the region, have traditionally provided an abundance of fish. Though not as well stocked today as they once were, classic Balkan cooking is proof of the wonderful variety of freshwater and ocean fish available from these natural sources. Carp is the predominant fish, but trout, swordfish and octopus are all popular. Many of these recipes rely on little more than herbs and spices, fresh vegetables or the local grain, mamaliga, to create quick, healthy and tasty meals.

Fish Baked in a Dough Jacket

In this traditional rural recipe, the whole fish is encased in a yeast-based dough, which traps all the juices and flavour.

INGREDIENTS

Serves 4–6
about 1kg/2¼lb whole fish, such as grey mullet, skinned and cleaned
flaked sea salt
sprigs of fennel, to garnish
lemon wedges and courgette and dill salad, to serve

For the dough
225g/8oz/2 cups strong white flour, sifted
1.5ml/¼ tsp salt
7g/¼oz sachet easy-blend dried yeast
1 egg, beaten
100–120ml/3½–4fl oz/⅓–½ cup milk and warm water combined

1 Preheat the oven to 180°C/350°F/ Gas 4. Pat the fish dry with kitchen paper and sprinkle inside and out with salt. Cover and chill the fish until the dough is ready for use.

2 Put the flour and salt into a large mixing bowl and stir in the yeast evenly. Make a well in the centre. Whisk together the egg, milk and water, then pour half into the centre of the flour. Knead to make a soft dough.

3 Knead the dough until smooth on a very lightly floured surface. Divide the dough into 2, making one portion slightly larger than the other.

4 Carefully roll out the smaller piece of dough on a lightly floured surface to the shape of your fish, allowing a 5cm/2in border. Lay the dough on a large greased shallow baking sheet. Place the fish on top.

5 Roll out the remaining piece of dough until large enough to cover the fish, again allowing for a 5cm/2in border. Brush the edges of the pastry with water and seal well. Make criss-cross patterns across the top, using a sharp knife. Leave to rise for 30 minutes.

6 Glaze the dough with the remaining egg mixture. Make a small hole in the top of the pastry to allow steam to escape. Bake the fish for 25–30 minutes or until golden brown and well risen. Garnish with sprigs of fennel and serve with wedges of lemon and a salad of finely sliced courgette, tossed in melted butter and sprinkled with dill seeds.

Swordfish Kebabs

Swordfish is a large ocean species found in Balkan waters, the Adriatic and the Black Seas. The firm, meaty flesh is ideal for charcoal grilling, poaching, steaming and baking.

INGREDIENTS

Serves 4

900g/2lb swordfish, skinned
5ml/1 tsp paprika, plus extra
  to garnish
60ml/4 tbsp lemon juice
45ml/3 tbsp olive oil
6 fresh bay leaves
4 small tomatoes
2 green peppers, seeded and cut into
  5cm/2in pieces
2 onions, cut into 4 wedges each
salt and freshly ground white pepper
extra bay leaves, to garnish
lettuce leaves, soured cream, cucumber
  salad and lime or lemon wedges,
  to serve

For the sauce

120ml/4fl oz/½ cup virgin olive oil
juice of 1 lemon
60ml/4 tbsp finely chopped
  fresh parsley
salt and freshly ground black pepper

3 Carefully turn the fish cubes in the marinade once or twice.

1 Cut the swordfish into 5cm/2in cubes and place in a shallow dish.

2 Mix together the paprika, lemon juice, olive oil and seasoning and pour over the fish. Crush 2 bay leaves over the fish. Leave, covered, in the refrigerator for at least 2 hours.

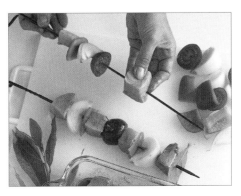

4 Thread the fish and vegetables on 4 large skewers; finish with a bay leaf.

5 Cook under a preheated grill or over the hot coals of a barbecue, basting with any remaining marinade mixture from time to time. Turn the fish once during cooking.

6 Meanwhile, for the sauce, in a bowl whisk the oil, lemon juice, parsley and seasoning together until emulsified (thickened) and pour into a jug. Arrange the kebabs on lettuce leaves and serve with the parsley oil sauce, soured cream sprinkled with paprika, a cucumber salad and lime or lemon wedges and garnish with extra bay leaves, if liked.

--- COOK'S TIP ---

To help prevent the onion from falling apart during the cooking, keep the root end intact when preparing the onion, so when you slice into it the root will hold the pieces together. Replace the swordfish with sturgeon, halibut or cod, if preferred.

Trout on a Grill

These days, rainbow trout is largely a farmed fish, though it naturally dwells in the rivers, streams and lakes of the Balkans. Its pretty pink flesh and strong flavour encourages a very simple approach, like this one, when it comes to cooking it.

INGREDIENTS

Serves 4
50g/2oz/4 tbsp butter, melted
5ml/1 tsp chopped fresh dill
5ml/1 tsp chopped fresh flat
 leaf parsley
4 trout fillets
45–60ml/3–4 tbsp lemon juice
salt and freshly ground black pepper
baby red Swiss chard leaves and sprigs
 of flat leaf parsley, to garnish

1 Stir together the butter, dill, flat leaf parsley and seasoning.

— COOK'S TIP —

If using a barbecue, put the fish in a double-sided, hinged basket, which allows you to turn the fish over easily. To prevent the head and tail from burning, brush with a little water then dip in granular salt.

2 Brush both sides of the fish with the herb butter before placing it under a preheated grill.

3 Grill for 5 minutes, then carefully turn over and cook the other side, basting with the remaining butter.

4 Just before serving, sprinkle over the lemon juice. Garnish with Swiss chard and sprigs of herbs.

Fish Parcels

Fish cooked in a parcel is a traditional method used by fishermen when cooking their lunch. They used to tie leaves or paper around the catch, dampen the parcel with water, bury it in hot ashes and cover it with a layer of hot coals.

INGREDIENTS

Serves 4
4 small seabass or trout, about
 400g/14oz each
juice of 1 lemon
50g/2oz/4 tbsp butter, melted
a few sprigs of parsley or dill
½ fennel bulb, cut into strips
salt and freshly ground black pepper or
 cayenne pepper
cornbread and tomato and cucumber
 salad, to serve

1 Preheat the oven to 180°C/350°F/ Gas 4, or light the barbecue. Remove the head, tail, fins and scales from the fish. Pat dry and season well. Sprinkle with lemon juice.

2 Cut out a double layer of greaseproof or parchment paper, large enough to put the fish into with enough extra to make a good seal. Brush the fish with the melted butter and place it in the centre. Sprinkle with half the parsley or dill and the fennel.

3 Wrap up the fish loosely to make a neat parcel. Press down the edges securely. Bake in the oven for about 15–20 minutes, depending on the thickness of the fish, or for 20–30 minutes if cooking on a barbecue.

4 Transfer the fish to serving plates and peel back the paper when ready to serve. Garnish with the remaining herbs and serve with slices of cornbread and a tomato and cucumber salad.

Onion and Fish Casserole

Choose a firm, white fish, such as cod or grey mullet, for this dish.

INGREDIENTS

Serves 4
45ml/3 tbsp olive oil
4 onions, finely chopped
5ml/1 tsp sea salt
45ml/3 tbsp water
3 garlic cloves, crushed
1 bay leaf
6 allspice berries
2.5ml/½ tsp paprika
4 plum tomatoes, seeded and diced
120ml/4fl oz/½ cup dry white wine,
   plus 45ml/3 tbsp
4 skinless fish steaks, about 175g/
   6oz each
lemon juice, for sprinkling
8 lemon slices
salt and freshly ground black pepper
15ml/1 tbsp chopped fresh parsley,
   to garnish
crusty bread, to serve

1 Preheat the oven to 180°C/350°F/ Gas 4. Put the oil, onion, sea salt and water in a heavy-based pan. Stir well and cook gently, covered, over a very low heat for 45 minutes but do not allow the onion to brown.

— COOK'S TIP —

For extra flavour, if you have time, marinate the fish in the salt, pepper and lemon juice for 1–2 hours in a covered, non-metallic bowl before cooking.

2 Stir in the garlic and cook for 1 minute before adding the bay leaf, allspice, paprika, tomatoes, the 120ml/4fl oz/½ cup wine and seasoning. Cook for 10–15 minutes, stirring occasionally to prevent sticking. Remove and discard the allspice and bay leaf.

3 Spoon a layer of the onion mixture into the base of a shallow ovenproof dish and top with the fish steaks. Sprinkle with a little lemon juice and seasoning.

4 Sprinkle over the remaining white wine and place two lemon slices overlapping on top of each fish steak. Spoon the remaining onion sauce over the fish.

5 Bake the casserole in the oven for 15–20 minutes, or until the sauce thickens and the fish flakes easily. Garnish with a sprinkling of parsley and serve with crusty bread.

Poached Carp with Caraway Seeds

Carp is a favourite freshwater fish in the Balkans as in Central Europe; not only is it plentiful but it is also easy to cook. This oil-rich fish dwells in the lakes and rivers and is generally sold alive in the local markets. Choose carp weighing 1.5–1.75kg/3–4lb, otherwise the fish tends to be coarse.

INGREDIENTS

Serves 4
4 carp fillets, about 175–200g/
   6–7oz each
15ml/1 tbsp caraway seeds,
   roughly crushed
40g/1½ oz/3 tbsp butter
30ml/2 tbsp snipped fresh chives
1 onion, finely sliced
juice of 1 lemon
175ml/6fl oz/¾ cup dry white wine
salt and freshly ground black pepper
dill and mint, to garnish
cornmeal porridge and green beans,
   to serve

1 Wipe the fish fillets and pat dry with kitchen paper. Season well and press the roughly crushed caraway seeds into the flesh.

2 Heat half the butter in a large frying pan and stir in half the fresh chives, the onion, lemon juice and dry white wine. Bring to the boil, reduce the heat and gently simmer for about 10–12 minutes.

3 Add the fish and poach gently for about 10 minutes. Carefully remove the fillets with a fish slice and keep them warm on a serving plate.

--- COOK'S TIP ---

The caraway seeds give the dish a very distinctive flavour, so be liberal with them.

4 Continue cooking the stock to reduce it a little, then whisk in the remaining butter. Adjust the seasoning. Pour the sauce over the fish and top with the remaining chives. Garnish with the herbs and serve with cornmeal porridge and green beans.

Fish Stew and Herby Mash

Use swordfish, sea bream, turbot, tuna or any firm fish with few bones. Serve hot or cold.

INGREDIENTS

Serves 4
45ml/3 tbsp olive oil
1 onion, finely chopped
2 garlic cloves, crushed
30ml/2 tbsp tomato purée
3 plum tomatoes, seeded and chopped
15ml/1 tbsp vinegar
1 bay leaf
15ml/1 tbsp chopped fresh flat
    leaf parsley
600ml/1 pint/2½ cups good
    fish stock
675–900g/1½–2lb mixed fish fillets,
    cut into 10cm/4in cubes
675g/1½lb old potatoes, peeled and
    cut into chunks
30ml/2 tbsp soured cream
salt and freshly ground black pepper
chopped fresh flat leaf parsley, bay
    leaves and grated lemon rind,
    to garnish

1 Heat the olive oil in a large pan, and cook the onion and garlic for 2–3 minutes or until just soft. Add the tomato purée, tomatoes, vinegar, bay leaf and parsley. Stir well before pouring in the fish stock. Bring to the boil.

COOK'S TIP

To make fish stock, place all the bones, trimmings, head and any leftover fish pieces in a large pan; add 1–2 carrots, 1 onion, sprigs of fennel or dill, a few peppercorns and a dash of dry white wine. Cover with cold water, bring to the boil then simmer for 20 minutes. Strain through a fine sieve.

2 Add the pieces of fish to the pan. Bring to the boil again, then reduce the heat and cook for approximately 30 minutes, stirring occasionally.

3 Meanwhile, place the potatoes in a large pan of lightly salted water. Bring to the boil and cook for 20 minutes. Drain well. Return to the pan, add the soured cream and a little pepper. Mash well with a fork.

4 Season the fish to taste. Serve with mashed potato on individual plates or in bowls. Garnish with the parsley and bay leaves and sprinkle grated lemon rind over the mash.

Mackerel in Wine Sauce

Dry white wine makes a good accompaniment to this fish.

INGREDIENTS

Serves 4
4 mackerel, filleted, with tails on
50ml/2fl oz/¼ cup olive oil
2 onions, finely sliced
3 garlic cloves, finely chopped
397g/14oz can plum tomatoes
250ml/8fl oz/1 cup dry white wine
salt and freshly ground black pepper
lemon slices, and parsley, to garnish
crusty rye bread, to serve

1 Preheat the oven to 200°C/400°F/ Gas 6. Pat the fish fillets dry with kitchen paper.

2 In a flameproof casserole heat the oil and cook the onions for 3–4 minutes or until soft. Stir in the garlic and cook for a further 2 minutes.

3 Spoon in the tomatoes and add the seasoning. Cook for 20 minutes.

4 Carefully add two of the mackerel fillets, skin side uppermost. Cook for 5 minutes on one side then remove and keep warm while you cook the remaining two mackerel. Using a fish slice, carefully transfer the four fillets to individual ovenproof dishes, the cooked side uppermost. Fold each fish loosely in half and pour in the tomato sauce, dividing it among the dishes.

5 Pour in the wine and cover each dish with foil. Cook in the oven for a further 25 minutes. Serve garnished with slices of lemon, sprigs of parsley and a little chopped parsley, accompanied by crusty rye bread.

Carp Stuffed with Walnuts

Serve this elaborate dish on
6 December for Saint Nikolas,
the patron saint of fishermen.

INGREDIENTS

Serves 10
about 1.5kg/3lb whole carp, scaled,
   cleaned and roe reserved
coarse sea salt

For the stuffing
175ml/6fl oz/³/₄ cup walnut oil
675g/1¹/₂lb onions, finely sliced
5ml/1 tsp paprika
pinch of cinnamon
175g/6oz/1¹/₂ cups walnuts, chopped
15ml/1 tbsp chopped fresh parsley
10ml/2 tsp fresh lemon juice
2 tomatoes, sliced
250ml/8fl oz/1 cup tomato juice
salt and freshly ground black pepper
walnuts and fennel sprigs, to garnish

1 Preheat the oven to 180°C/350°F/
Gas 4. Sprinkle the inside of the
fish with a little sea salt.

2 In a frying pan, heat the oil then
cook the onions, paprika and
cinnamon together until soft.

3 Remove any membrane or skin
from the roe and roughly chop.

4 Add the roe and walnuts to the
frying pan and cook, stirring all
the time, for 5−6 minutes. Leave to
cool before stirring in the parsley and
lemon juice. Season to taste.

5 Fill the cavity of the fish with half
of the filling and secure with
cocktail sticks. Spoon the remaining
stuffing into the base of an ovenproof
dish and then place the fish on top.

6 Arrange the sliced tomatoes over
the top of the fish and spoon over
the tomato juice. Bake in the oven for
30–45 minutes, or until the fish is
browned and flakes easily.

7 Carefully transfer to a serving plate.
Discard the cocktail sticks before
serving the fish sprinkled with extra
walnut pieces and sprigs of fennel.

Stuffed Red Snapper

There are a number of local flavours combined in this unusual recipe – the red snapper filled with carp, sharpened by the salty cheese and dill pickle.

INGREDIENTS

Serves 4
4 small red snapper, about 450g/1lb
    each, filleted and heads and
    fins removed
juice of 1 lemon
350g/12oz fish fillets, such as carp,
    pike or sole, skinned
1 egg white
2.5ml/½ tsp chopped fresh tarragon
1 dill pickle, sliced
40g/1½oz/¾ cup fresh breadcrumbs
40g/1½oz/¼ cup feta cheese or
    brinza, roughly crumbled
salt and freshly ground white pepper
25g/1oz/2 tbsp butter, melted
sprigs of tarragon or sweet cicely plus
    pansies or other edible flowers,
    to garnish
lemon wedges, to serve

1 Preheat the oven to 180°C/350°F/ Gas 4. Wipe out the snapper and pat dry, removing any membrane with a little salt. Liberally rub the lemon juice inside the fish.

2 Put the fish fillets in a food processor and process with the egg white, tarragon, dill pickle, bread-crumbs, cheese and a little ground white pepper, until a smooth paste is formed for the stuffing.

3 Using a spoon, fill the fish with the fish fillet mixture and lay them in an ovenproof dish.

4 Secure the fish with wooden satay sticks and bake for 40–50 minutes. Spoon over the melted butter halfway through cooking.

5 Transfer the fish carefully to a serving plate. Serve with lemon wedges and garnish with fresh sprigs of tarragon or sweet cicely and edible flowers, if liked.

VEGETABLES AND GRAINS

Aubergines, courgettes, capsicum, cucumbers and tomatoes are just some of the vegetables that are available fresh in the Balkan markets. While some of the recipes in this section reflect Italian, Turkish or Greek influences, such as Courgettes with Rice and Stuffed Vine Leaves, others are uniquely Balkan. Mamaliga Baked with Cheese, using the local grain, mamaliga, is a perfect example of the versatility of this staple ingredient. The excellent shopska salads featuring the local yogurt are another typical delight.

Creamy Aubergine and Mushrooms

This traditional way to serve aubergines may seem unusual to Western cooks, but is based on typical ingredients of the area.

INGREDIENTS

Serves 4–6
2 aubergines
115g/4oz/½ cup unsalted butter
225g/8oz/3 cups mushrooms, sliced
120ml/4fl oz/½ cup good strong
   beef stock
250ml/8fl oz/1 cup double cream
60ml/4 tbsp chopped fresh parsley
salt and freshly ground white pepper
soured cream, to serve (optional)

1 Peel the aubergines with a sharp knife then slice into 7.5cm/3in long sticks, about 5mm/¼in thick.

2 Put the aubergine on a dish towel and sprinkle liberally with salt.

3 Fold over the dish cloth to cover the aubergine and leave for 30–35 minutes. Use the cloth to squeeze out the moisture from the aubergine.

4 Heat the butter in a large frying pan and cook the aubergine and mushrooms for 10 minutes. Pour in the beef stock and simmer for a further 15 minutes, stirring occasionally.

5 Season to taste before stirring in the cream. Reheat but do not allow to boil. Add 45ml/3 tbsp of the parsley and stir well. Spoon into a warm serving dish and garnish with the remaining parsley. Serve with soured cream, if liked.

COOK'S TIP

For a really smooth vegetable dish, carefully blend together the aubergine and mushrooms in a food processor or blender after the initial 10 minutes of cooking. Add the beef stock and follow the rest of the recipe.

Courgettes with Rice

This dish bears testimony to the influence of Italy, just on the other side of the Adriatic Sea, on Balkan cuisine.

INGREDIENTS

Serves 4 as a main course
8 as a side dish

1kg/2¼lb small or medium courgettes
60ml/4 tbsp olive oil
3 onions, finely chopped
3 garlic cloves, crushed
5ml/1 tsp chilli powder
397g/14oz can chopped tomatoes
200g/7oz/1 cup risotto or round
  grain rice
600–750ml/1–1¼ pints/2½–3 cups
  vegetable or chicken stock
30ml/2 tbsp chopped fresh parsley
30ml/2 tbsp chopped fresh dill
salt and freshly ground white pepper
sprigs of dill and olives, to garnish
thick natural yogurt, to serve

1 Preheat the oven to 190°C/375°F/ Gas 5. Top and tail the courgettes and slice into large chunks.

2 Heat half the olive oil in a large pan and gently fry the onions and garlic until just soft. Stir in the chilli powder and tomatoes and simmer for about 5–8 minutes before adding the courgettes and salt to taste.

COOK'S TIP

Add extra liquid as necessary, during step 5, to prevent the mixture from sticking.

3 Cook over a gentle to medium heat for 10–15 minutes, before stirring the rice into the pan.

4 Add the stock to the pan, cover and simmer for about 45 minutes or until the rice is tender. Stir the mixture occasionally.

5 Remove from the heat and stir in pepper to taste, parsley and dill. Spoon into an ovenproof dish and bake for about 45 minutes.

6 Halfway through cooking, brush the remaining oil over the courgette mixture. Garnish with the dill and olives. Serve with the yogurt.

Thracian Tomato Casserole

This is a typical recipe from the Thracian region of southern Bulgaria. It is eaten at harvest time during the hottest days of the year.

INGREDIENTS

Serves 4
40ml/2½ tbsp olive oil
45ml/3 tbsp chopped fresh flat
    leaf parsley
1kg/2¼lb firm ripe tomatoes
5ml/1 tsp caster sugar
40g/1½oz/scant 1 cup day-old
    breadcrumbs
2.5ml/½ tsp chilli powder
    or paprika
salt
chopped parsley, to garnish
rye bread, to serve

1 Preheat the oven to 200°C/400°F/ Gas 6. Brush a large baking dish with 15ml/1 tbsp of the oil.

2 Sprinkle the chopped flat leaf parsley over the base of the dish. Cut the tomatoes into even slices, discarding the two end slices of each. Arrange the slices of tomato in the dish so that they overlap slightly. Sprinkle them with a little salt and the caster sugar.

VARIATION

To vary this recipe, replace half the quantity of tomatoes with 450g/1lb courgettes. Slice the courgettes evenly and arrange alternate slices of courgette and tomato in the dish, overlapping the slices as before.

3 In a mixing bowl, stir together the breadcrumbs, the remaining oil and chilli powder or paprika, then sprinkle over the top of the tomatoes.

4 Bake in the oven for 40–50 minutes, covering with foil if the topping is getting too brown. Serve hot or cold, garnished with chopped parsley and accompanied by rye bread.

Mixed Vegetable Casserole

INGREDIENTS

Serves 4
1 aubergine
115g/4oz/½ cup okra, halved
    lengthways
225g/8oz/2 cups frozen or fresh peas
225g/8oz/1½ cups green beans, cut
    into 2.5cm/1in pieces
4 courgettes, cut into 1cm/½in pieces
2 onions, finely chopped
450g/1lb old potatoes, diced into
    2.5cm/1in pieces
1 red pepper, seeded and sliced
397g/14oz can chopped tomatoes
150ml/¼ pint/⅔ cup vegetable stock
60ml/4 tbsp olive oil
75ml/5 tbsp chopped fresh parsley
5ml/1 tsp paprika
salt

For the topping
3 tomatoes, sliced
1 courgette, sliced

1 Preheat the oven to 190°C/375°F/ Gas 5. Dice the aubergine into 2.5cm/1in pieces. Add the vegetables to a large ovenproof casserole.

2 Stir in the canned tomatoes, stock, olive oil, parsley, paprika and salt to taste. Stir well.

3 Level the surface of the vegetables and arrange alternate slices of tomatoes and courgette attractively on top.

4 Put the lid on or cover the casserole dish tightly. Cook for 60–70 minutes. Serve either hot or cold with wedges of crusty bread.

Stuffed Vine Leaves

This vegetarian version of the famous Greek dish uses rice, pine nuts and raisins.

INGREDIENTS

Makes about 40
40 fresh vine leaves
60ml/4 tbsp olive oil
lemon wedges and a crisp salad,
  to serve

For the stuffing
150g/5oz/³/₄ cup long grain
  rice, rinsed
2 bunches spring onions,
  finely chopped
40g/1¹/₂oz/¹/₄ cup pine nuts
25g/1oz/scant ¹/₄ cup seedless raisins
30ml/2 tbsp chopped fresh mint leaves
60ml/4 tbsp chopped fresh parsley
3.5ml/³/₄ tsp freshly ground
  black pepper
salt

1 Using a knife or a pair of scissors, snip out the thick, coarse stems from the vine leaves. Blanch the leaves in a large pan of boiling salted water until they just begin to change colour. Drain and refresh in cold water.

2 Mix all the stuffing ingredients together in a bowl.

3 Open out the vine leaves, ribbed side uppermost. Place a heaped teaspoonful of the stuffing on each.

--- COOK'S TIP ---

When fresh vine leaves are unavailable, use 2 packets of vine leaves preserved in brine and rinse then drain well before using.

4 Fold over the two outer edges to prevent the stuffing from falling out, then roll up the vine leaf from the stem end to form a neat roll.

5 Arrange the stuffed vine leaves neatly in a steamer and sprinkle over the olive oil. Cook over steam for 50–60 minutes, or until the rice is completely cooked. Serve with lemon wedges and a salad, either cold as a *meze* or hot as a starter to a meal.

Stuffed Celeriac

Rather odd-looking, celeriac is a root vegetable that resembles an underdeveloped head of celery, and tastes a bit like sweet, nutty celery. It can be boiled in water or stock, and in this Romanian recipe, it is cooked in a mixture of olive oil and lemon-flavoured water, giving it extra zest.

INGREDIENTS

Serves 4
4 small celeriac, about 200–225g/
   7–8oz each
juice of 2 lemons
150ml/¼ pint/⅔ cup extra virgin
   olive oil
lemon wedges and sprigs of flat leaf
   parsley, to garnish

For the stuffing
6 garlic cloves, finely chopped
5ml/1 tsp black peppercorns,
   finely crushed
60–75ml/4–5 tbsp chopped
   fresh parsley
salt

1 Peel the celeriac carefully with a sharp knife and quickly immerse in a bowl of water and the lemon juice until ready to use.

COOK'S TIP

It is necessary to add the lemon juice to the water in order to help prevent the peeled celeriac discolouring.

2 Reserve the lemon water. Very carefully scoop out the flesh of each celeriac, leaving a shell about 2cm/¾in thick, in which to put the filling.

3 Working quickly, chop up the scooped out celeriac flesh and mix with the garlic and peppercorns. Add the parsley and season with salt.

4 Fill the shells with the stuffing and sit them in a large pan, making sure they remain upright throughout cooking. Pour in the olive oil and enough lemon water to come halfway up the celeriac.

5 Simmer very gently until the celeriac are tender and nearly all the cooking liquid has been absorbed. Serve the celeriac hot or cold with their juices, and garnish with lemon wedges and sprigs of parsley.

Green Bean Stew

Paprika was originally taken to Hungary by the Turks, so it is not surprising to find it used in many Balkan dishes. Its mild, slightly bitter spiciness combines well with fresh vegetables, such as tomatoes and beans.

INGREDIENTS

Serves 4–6
900g/2lb/6 cups young green beans
45ml/3 tbsp olive or vegetable oil
3 onions, finely diced
350g/12oz fresh plum tomatoes, roughly chopped
5ml/1 tsp paprika
6 garlic cloves, crushed
30ml/2 tbsp chopped fresh flat leaf parsley
salt and freshly ground black pepper
a little chopped fresh parsley and paprika, to garnish

1 Top and tail the beans and cut into 4cm/1½in lengths. Tip the beans into a pan of boiling water. Quickly bring back to the boil, then reduce the heat to a simmer. Cook until just softened, about 5 minutes. Drain well and keep warm.

2 Meanwhile, heat the oil in a pan and fry the onions until just starting to turn a pale golden colour.

3 Add the tomatoes and paprika to the onions, then stir in the green beans. Simmer with the lid on for 10–15 minutes, then stir in the garlic and parsley. Season to taste and serve the beans garnished with a sprinkle of paprika and some parsley.

> ——— COOK'S TIP ———
>
> Make sure the beans are stringless or the quality of the dish will be spoiled.

Green Peas with Bacon

Historically, most rural families in Eastern Europe would have kept a pig and cured every part of it to provide food all year round. Versatile and full of flavour, bacon gives a boost to the simplest of dishes.

INGREDIENTS

Serves 4–6
450g/1lb/4 cups fresh peas
pinch of granulated sugar
30ml/2 tbsp vegetable oil
1 onion, finely chopped
2 red chillies, seeded and finely chopped
75g/3oz lean bacon, finely chopped
3 firm ripe tomatoes, finely chopped
salt and freshly ground black pepper
pickled red chillies, to garnish

1 Cook the peas in plenty of boiling salted water with the pinch of sugar, for 6–8 minutes. Drain well.

2 Meanwhile, heat the oil in a frying pan and cook the onion and chillies until just pale golden brown. Add the bacon and continue to fry together for a further 4–5 minutes, stirring well.

3 Add the chopped tomatoes and cook for a further 2–3 minutes over a gentle heat. Stir in the peas and reheat. Season to taste. Put the peas in a hot serving dish and garnish with pickled red chillies.

Mamaliga Baked with Cheese

Mamaliga, the local cornmeal, is first cooked to a porridge-like consistency, then baked with feta and the local cheese, *kashkaval*, to give it a pleasantly sharp taste.

INGREDIENTS

Serves 4–6

130g/4¹/₂oz/generous 1 cup
    coarse ground cornmeal
1 litre/1³/₄ pints/4 cups water
50g/2oz/4 tbsp unsalted butter
350g/12oz/1¹/₂ cups feta cheese or
    brinza, drained and crumbled
50g/2oz/¹/₂ cup hard *kashkaval* cheese,
    grated, for sprinkling
salt and freshly ground black pepper
grilled bacon and spring onions, sliced
    lengthways, to garnish
tomato sauce, to serve

1 Preheat the oven to 190°C/375°F/ Gas 5. Stirring occasionally, dry fry the cornmeal in a large pan for 3–4 minutes, or until it changes colour. Remove from the heat.

2 Slowly pour in the water and add a little salt. Return the pan to the heat and stir well until the cornmeal thickens a little. Cover, reduce the heat and leave for 25 minutes to cook, stirring often.

3 Remove from the heat when thick enough to cause a wide trail to be left when a wooden spoon is lifted from the mixture. Stir in the butter, feta cheese or *brinza* and season well.

4 Spoon into a 20cm/8in greased springform tin. Bake for 25–30 minutes or until firm. Leave overnight or for 2–3 hours. Serve sprinkled with *kashkaval* cheese, bacon and spring onions, with tomato sauce.

Mamaliga Balls

Popular snack food, the *mamaliga* balls in this recipe contain bite-sized pieces of salami, but chunks of smoked ham or cheese is equally suitable.

INGREDIENTS

Serves 6–8

250g/9oz/generous 2 cups
    fine cornmeal
600ml/1 pint/2¹/₂ cups lightly
    salted water
generous knob of butter
115g/4oz/1 cup salami, roughly
    chopped
oil, for deep-fat frying
salt and freshly ground black pepper
pan-fried tomatoes and chopped fresh
    herbs, to serve

1 Stir the cornmeal and water together in a heavy-based saucepan. Bring to the boil and, stirring all the time, cook for 12 minutes, or until suitable for rolling into balls. Stir in the butter and season well.

2 With lightly floured hands, roll the balls to double the size of a walnut and place the salami in the middle before rolling up.

3 Fry the balls in the oil at 180–190°C/350–375°F, for 2–3 minutes or until golden brown. Drain well on kitchen paper. Serve with pan-fried tomatoes and chopped herbs.

> ——— COOK'S TIP ———
>
> *Mamaliga* is available in several grades, from coarse to fine. Coarse stoneground is often the best type for cooking.

Baked Cabbage

This economical dish uses the whole cabbage, including the core where much flavour resides.

INGREDIENTS

Serves 4

1 green or white cabbage, about
   675g/1½lb
15ml/1 tbsp light olive oil
30ml/2 tbsp water
45–60ml/3–4 tbsp vegetable stock
4 firm, ripe tomatoes, peeled
   and chopped
5ml/1 tsp mild chilli powder
salt
15ml/1 tbsp chopped fresh parsley or
   fennel, to garnish, optional

For the topping
3 firm ripe tomatoes, thinly sliced
15ml/1 tbsp olive oil
salt and freshly ground black pepper

1 Preheat the oven to 180°C/350°F/ Gas 4. Finely shred the leaves and the core of the cabbage. Heat the oil in a frying pan with the water and add the cabbage. Cook over a very low heat, to allow the cabbage to sweat, for about 5–10 minutes with the lid on. Stir occasionally.

2 Add the stock and stir in the tomatoes. Cook for a further 10 minutes. Season with the chilli powder and a little salt.

3 Tip the cabbage mixture into the base of an ovenproof dish. Level the surface of the cabbage and arrange the sliced tomatoes on top. Season and brush with the oil to prevent them drying out. Cook for 30–40 minutes, or until the tomatoes are just starting to brown. Serve hot, garnished with a little parsley or fennel sprinkled over the top, if liked.

COOK'S TIPS

To vary the taste, add seeded, diced red or green peppers to the cabbage with the tomatoes. If you have a shallow flameproof casserole, you could cook the cabbage in it on the hob and then simply transfer the casserole to the oven for baking.

Creamed Courgettes

Like aubergines, courgettes are another versatile vegetable. For extra texture and crunch the courgette in this recipe is covered in a light sprinkling of breadcrumbs before grilling.

INGREDIENTS

Serves 4–6
6 courgettes, about 200g/7oz each
65g/2½oz/5 tbsp unsalted butter
1 onion, finely chopped
60ml/4 tbsp day-old breadcrumbs
salt
olives, lemon slices and sprig of
  parsley, to garnish

1 Trim the courgettes and cut into 1cm/½in slices. Add to a pan of boiling water and cook for 5–8 minutes, or until just tender. Drain very well.

2 Using a potato masher, mash the courgettes or blend in a food processor or blender until smooth.

3 Melt 40g/1½oz/3 tbsp of the butter in a frying pan and cook the onion until soft, then stir in the puréed courgettes. Cook without browning for a further 2–3 minutes, before spooning into a warm ovenproof serving dish.

4 Dot the courgette with the remaining butter and sprinkle over the breadcrumbs. Cook under a preheated grill until golden brown. Garnish with olives, lemon slices and a sprig of parsley just before serving.

— COOK'S TIP —

As an alternative, replace the courgettes with two large marrows that have been peeled, seeded and diced.

Cucumber and Tomato Salad

This Bulgarian *shopska* salad uses the excellent local yogurt. It is claimed that yogurt originated in Bulgaria. If unavailable, use a Greek-style yogurt instead.

INGREDIENTS

Serves 4
450g/1lb firm ripe tomatoes
½ cucumber
1 onion

For the dressing
60ml/4 tbsp olive or vegetable oil
90ml/6 tbsp thick Greek-style yogurt
30ml/2 tbsp chopped fresh parsley
   or chives
2.5ml/½ tsp vinegar
salt and freshly ground black pepper
1 small hot chilli, seeded and chopped,
   or 2.5cm/1in lengths of chives,
   to garnish
country bread, to serve

1 Skin the tomatoes by first cutting a cross in the base of each tomato. Place in a bowl and cover with boiling water for 1–2 minutes, or until the skin starts to split, then drain and plunge into cold water. Cut the tomatoes into quarters, seed and chop.

2 Chop the cucumber and onion into pieces the same size as the tomatoes and put them all in a bowl.

3 Mix all the dressing ingredients together and season to taste. Pour over the salad and toss all the ingredients together. Sprinkle over black pepper and the chopped chilli or chives to garnish and serve with crusty bread.

Black Olive and Sardine Salad

The combined ingredients – sardines, olives, tomatoes and wine vinegar – bring a real burst of flavour to a delightful light summer salad.

INGREDIENTS

Serves 6
8 large firm ripe tomatoes
1 large red onion
60ml/4 tbsp wine vinegar
90ml/6 tbsp good olive oil
18–24 small sardines, cooked
75g/3oz/¾ cup black pitted olives,
   drained well
salt and freshly ground black pepper
45ml/3 tbsp chopped fresh parsley,
   to garnish

1 Slice the tomatoes into 5mm/¼in slices. Slice the onion thinly.

2 Arrange the tomatoes on a serving plate, overlapping the slices, then top with the red onion.

3 Mix together the wine vinegar, olive oil and seasoning and spoon over the tomatoes.

4 Top with the sardines and black olives and sprinkle the chopped parsley over the top.

COOK'S TIP

This recipe works equally well if the sardines are replaced with 6 shelled and halved hard-boiled eggs.

DESSERTS AND BAKES

There is a wonderful choice of puddings and desserts within the Balkan countries, ranging from simple Baked Peaches with cream to rich chocolate tortes, such as Torte Varazdin. Fresh fruit and nuts, such as walnuts and chestnuts, are popular ingredients and are often combined with sugar or honey to make sweet pastry desserts. However, locally produced rose petals and rose water – simply served swirled through a rice pudding for example – are perhaps the most distinctive addition to Balkan desserts.

Walnut and Coffee Slice

This two-layered slice has a rich walnut base and a creamy light coffee topping. Serve with a complementary drink such as a sour cherry liqueur.

INGREDIENTS

Serves 8–12
4 sheets of filo pastry
50g/2oz/4 tbsp unsalted butter, melted
4 eggs, separated
175g/6oz/scant 1 cup caster sugar
90g/3½oz/scant 1 cup walnuts, finely ground
walnut pieces and sifted icing sugar, to decorate

For the topping
200g/7oz/scant 1 cup unsalted butter, at room temperature
1 egg yolk
150g/5oz/¾ cup caster sugar
45ml/3 tbsp cold strong coffee

1 Preheat the oven to 180°C/350°F/ Gas 4. Grease and line a deep 20cm/8in square cake tin. Brush the sheets of filo pastry with the butter, fold them over and place in the base of the prepared tin.

COOK'S TIPS

Please note this recipe contains raw egg yolk. Use pistachios in place of the walnuts if preferred, grinding them in a processor.

2 Whisk the egg yolks and sugar in a mixing bowl until thick and pale, and the whisk leaves a trail.

3 Whisk the egg whites until stiff. Fold in the ground nuts.

4 Fold the egg white into the egg yolk mixture. Spoon into the prepared tin. Bake for about 25–30 minutes, until firm. Allow to cool.

5 Meanwhile, for the topping, cream the ingredients well. Spread on the cake with a round-bladed knife. Scatter over the walnut pieces. Chill for at least 3–4 hours or overnight. Sprinkle with icing sugar and cut into fingers, triangles or squares.

Torte Varazdin

The classic chocolate cake is a favourite world-wide, and appears in many guises. In this version from the former Yugoslavia, it is enhanced with a creamy chestnut filling.

INGREDIENTS

Serves 8–12

225g/8oz/1 cup butter, at
　room temperature
225g/8oz/generous 1 cup caster sugar
200g/7oz plain chocolate, melted
6 eggs, separated
130g/4½oz/generous 1 cup plain
　flour, sifted
chocolate curls, to decorate

For the filling

250ml/8fl oz/1 cup double cream,
　lightly whipped
450g/1lb/1¾ cups canned
　chestnut purée
115g/4oz/generous ½ cup caster sugar

For the topping

150g/5oz/10 tbsp unsalted butter
150g/5oz/1¼ cups icing sugar, sifted
115g/4oz plain chocolate, melted

1 Preheat the oven to 180°C/350°F/
Gas 4. Grease and line the base and sides of a 20–23cm/8–9in round cake tin. Cream the butter and sugar together in a bowl until pale and fluffy. Stir in the melted chocolate and egg yolks. Fold the flour carefully into the chocolate mixture.

2 In a grease-free bowl whisk the egg whites until stiff. Add a spoonful of the egg white to the chocolate mixture to loosen it, then carefully fold in the remainder. Spoon the cake mixture into the prepared tin.

3 Bake the cake for 45–50 minutes, or until firm to the touch and a skewer inserted into the middle comes out clean. Cool on a wire rack. When cold, peel off the lining paper and slice the cake in half horizontally.

4 Meanwhile, gently mix the filling ingredients together in a bowl. Sandwich the two cake halves together firmly with the chestnut filling.

5 In a mixing bowl, cream together the butter and sugar for the topping before stirring in the melted chocolate. Using a dampened knife spread the chocolate topping over the sides and top of the cake. Chill for 60 minutes before serving if possible, decorated with chocolate curls.

Baklava

The origins of this recipe are in Greece and Turkey, but it has been willingly adopted throughout south-eastern Europe. It is a very sweet dessert and black coffee is the perfect accompaniment.

INGREDIENTS

Makes 24 pieces
175g/6oz/³/₄ cup butter, melted
400g/14oz packet filo pastry, thawed
    if frozen
30ml/2 tbsp lemon juice
60ml/4 tbsp clear thick honey
50g/2oz/¹/₄ cup caster sugar
finely grated rind of 1 lemon
10ml/2 tsp cinnamon
200g/7oz/1³/₄ cups blanched
    almonds, chopped
200g/7oz/1³/₄ cups walnuts, chopped
75g/3oz/³/₄ cup pistachios or
    hazelnuts, chopped
chopped pistachios, to decorate

For the syrup
350g/12oz/1³/₄ cups caster sugar
115g/4oz/¹/₂ cup clear honey
600ml/1 pint/2¹/₂ cups water
2 strips of thinly pared lemon rind

1 Preheat the oven to 160°C/325°F/ Gas 3. Brush the base of a shallow 30 × 20cm/12 × 8in loose-bottomed or Swiss roll tin with a little of the melted butter.

2 Using the tin as a guide cut the sheets of filo pastry with a sharp knife to fit the tin exactly.

3 Place one sheet of pastry in the base of the tin, brush with a little melted butter, then repeat until you have used half of the pastry sheets. Set the remaining pastry aside and cover with a clean dish towel.

4 To make the filling, place the lemon juice, honey and sugar in a pan and heat gently until dissolved. Stir in the lemon rind, cinnamon and chopped nuts. Mix thoroughly.

5 Spread half the filling over the pastry, cover with 3 layers of the filo pastry and butter then spread the remaining filling over the pastry.

6 Finish by using up the remaining sheets of pastry and butter on top, and brush the top of the pastry liberally with butter.

7 Using a sharp knife, carefully mark the pastry into squares, almost cutting through the filling. Bake in the preheated oven for 1 hour, or until crisp and golden brown.

8 Meanwhile, make the syrup. Place the caster sugar, honey, water and lemon rind in a pan and stir over a low heat until the sugar and honey have dissolved. Bring to the boil, then boil for a further 10 minutes until the mixture has thickened slightly.

9 Take the syrup off the heat and leave to cool slightly. Remove the baklava from the oven. Remove and discard the lemon rind from the syrup then pour over the pastry. Leave to soak for 6 hours or overnight. Cut into squares and serve, decorated with chopped pistachios.

Currant Apple Mousse

This Romanian recipe uses locally grown apples and currants, macerated in red wine, to make this creamy mousse.

INGREDIENTS

Serves 4–6

175g/6oz/³⁄₄ cup currants
175ml/6fl oz/³⁄₄ cup red wine, plus
　a little extra for topping up
4 crisp eating apples, cored, peeled
　and sliced
250ml/8fl oz/1 cup water
225g/8oz/generous 1 cup
　caster sugar
30ml/2 tbsp cornflour
few drops of pink food
　colouring (optional)
3 egg yolks
5ml/1 tsp vanilla essence
1.5ml/¹⁄₄ tsp cinnamon
2 egg whites
seedless black grapes, a little caster
　sugar and mint leaves,
　to decorate

1 Soak the currants in the red wine for 1–1¹⁄₂ hours. Drain the currants and set aside. Strain the wine through a fine sieve, to remove most of the currant bits, then top up with more wine as necessary to bring back up to 175ml/6fl oz/³⁄₄ cup.

2 While the currants are soaking, put the apples in a pan and cook with the water and three-quarters of the caster sugar until soft. Leave to cool.

3 Purée the apples in a processor and then return to the pan.

4 Blend together the cornflour and the red wine and then pour into the apple purée. Cook for about 8–10 minutes, stirring all the time. Add the food colouring, if using.

5 Beat the egg yolks in a bowl with the remaining caster sugar and the vanilla essence until pale and thick.

6 Whisk the apple mixture slowly into the egg yolks. Add the cinnamon and beat until smooth.

7 Refrigerate until thickened. Reserve 5ml/1 tsp of the egg white for decorating and whisk the remainder in a grease-free bowl, until stiff. Fold the currants and the whisked egg whites into the apple mixture and chill well.

8 While the mousse is chilling, make the frosted grapes. Brush the grapes with a little of the reserved egg white and sprinkle with caster sugar. Leave to dry. Use with the mint leaves to decorate the mousse.

Cherry Strudel

There are many varieties of strudel filling in this region, ranging from poppy seed, raisin and honey to sweet cheese. Cherry or apple strudels are among the most popular. A true strudel pastry is very thin, light and crispy, and takes a long time to roll out; nevertheless, it really is worth the effort.

INGREDIENTS

Serves 8–10
250g/9oz/2¹/₄ cups strong flour
75g/3oz/²/₃ cup plain flour
1 egg, beaten
150g/5oz/10 tbsp butter, melted
100ml/3¹/₂ fl oz/¹/₂ cup warm water
sifted icing sugar, for dredging

For the filling
65g/2¹/₂ oz/generous ¹/₂ cup walnuts,
   roughly chopped
115g/4oz/generous ¹/₂ cup caster sugar
675g/1¹/₂ lb cherries, stoned
40g/1¹/₂ oz/scant 1 cup day-old
   breadcrumbs

1 Preheat the oven to 200°C/400°F/ Gas 6. Sift the flours together in a warm bowl. Make a well in the centre, add the egg, 115g/4oz/¹/₂ cup of the melted butter and the water. Mix to a smooth pliable dough, adding a little extra flour if required. Leave wrapped in clear film for 30 minutes to rest.

2 Meanwhile in a large bowl, mix together the chopped walnuts, sugar, cherries and breadcrumbs.

3 Lay out a clean dish towel and sprinkle it with flour. Carefully roll out the dough until it covers the towel. The dough should be as thin as possible, so that you can see the design on the cloth through it.

4 Dampen the edges with water. Spread the cherry filling over the pastry, leaving a gap all the way round the edge, about 2.5cm/1in wide. Roll up the pastry carefully with the side edges folded in over the filling to prevent it coming out. Use the dish towel to help you roll the pastry.

5 Brush the strudel with the remaining melted butter. Place on a baking sheet and curl into a horseshoe shape. Cook for 30–40 minutes, or until golden brown. Dredge with icing sugar; serve warm or cold.

Boyer Cream

This light and fluffy mousse-like dessert is flavoured with a hint of rose water.

INGREDIENTS

Serves 4–6
225g/8oz/1 cup full-fat cream cheese
75ml/5 tbsp soured cream
2 eggs, separated
50g/2oz/¼ cup vanilla sugar
115g/4oz/²⁄₃ cup raspberries
115g/4oz/1 cup strawberries
sifted icing sugar, to taste
15ml/1 tbsp rose water
halved strawberries, mint leaves and
    small pink roses, to decorate

1 Beat the cream cheese in a bowl with the soured cream and egg yolks until the cheese has softened. Stir in half the sugar.

2 Whisk the egg whites in another bowl until stiff, then whisk in the remaining sugar. Fold the egg whites into the cream cheese mixture. Chill until ready for use.

3 To make the fruit sauce, purée the raspberries and strawberries. Sieve to remove pips; add icing sugar, to taste. Swirl 4–6 glass dishes with a little rose water and divide three-quarters of the sauce between the dishes. Top with the cream cheese mixture. Add the remaining sauce in spoonfuls, swirling it into the cream cheese.

4 Place the dishes on saucers and decorate with halved strawberries, mint leaves and small roses.

Bulgarian Rice Pudding

There are many versions of rice pudding to choose from, but the presence here of pistachios, lemon, cinnamon and rose petals, makes this version a distinctly Bulgarian one.

INGREDIENTS

Serves 4–6
75g/3oz/scant ½ cup short-grain
    or pudding rice
45ml/3 tbsp granulated sugar
900ml/1½ pints/3¾ cups full-
    cream milk
25g/1oz/2 tbsp unsalted butter
1 cinnamon stick
strip of lemon rind
halved pistachios and rose petals,
    to decorate

1 Put the rice, sugar, milk, butter, cinnamon stick and lemon rind into a large double or heavy-based pan.

COOK'S TIP

For an extra creamy rice pudding, fold in 150ml/¼ pint/⅔ cup lightly whipped double cream, just before serving.

2 Cook over a very gentle heat, stirring occasionally, for about 1½ hours, or until thick and creamy. Remove and discard the cinnamon stick and lemon rind.

3 Spoon into serving dishes and sprinkle with halved pistachios and rose petals, to decorate.

Lemon Cake

This simple, pleasing Romanian cake is made from a blend of thick yogurt, lemon and honey, with a hint of cinnamon.

INGREDIENTS

Makes 16

50g/2oz/4 tbsp butter, softened
115g/4oz/generous ½ cup caster sugar
2 large eggs, separated
115g/4oz/½ cup Greek yogurt
grated rind of 2 lemons
juice of ½ lemon
150g/5oz/1¼ cups self-raising flour
2.5ml/½ tsp baking powder
curls of lemon rind, to decorate

For the syrup

juice of ½ lemon
60ml/4 tbsp honey
45ml/3 tbsp water
1 small cinnamon stick

1 Preheat the oven to 190°C/375°F/ Gas 5. Grease and line a shallow 18cm/7in square cake tin. Cream together the softened butter and sugar in a bowl until pale and fluffy.

2 Slowly add the egg yolks, Greek yogurt and lemon rind and juice. Beat until smooth. In a separate, grease-free bowl, whisk the egg whites until just stiff.

3 Sift together the flour and baking powder. Fold into the yogurt mixture, then fold in the egg whites.

4 Spoon the mixture into the prepared cake tin. Bake for about 25 minutes, or until golden brown and firm to the touch. Turn out on to a plate and peel off the base paper.

5 Meanwhile, to make the syrup, put the lemon juice, honey, water and cinnamon stick together in a small pan. Stir until boiling then cook until the mixture is syrupy.

6 Remove the pan from the heat. Remove and discard the cinnamon stick. Spoon the warm syrup over the cake, then sprinkle with the lemon rind. Leave to cool completely before cutting into 16 pieces.

COOK'S TIP

The local honey has a perfumed flavour due to the pollen collected from the wild plants in the foothills of the fruit orchards. Try and use scented honey in this dish.

Citrus Ricotta Squares

This light cheese cake has a sponge layer top and bottom and a creamy ricotta cheese filling with a hint of citrus.

INGREDIENTS

Makes 16

3 large eggs, separated
175g/6oz/scant 1 cup caster sugar
45ml/3 tbsp hot water
185g/6½oz/1⅔ cups plain flour, sifted
2.5ml/½ tsp baking powder
icing sugar, sifted, for dredging
long strands of lemon rind,
    to decorate
fresh fruit, to serve

For the filling

500g/1¼lb/2½ cups ricotta cheese
100ml/3½fl oz/½ cup double cream,
    lightly whipped
25g/1oz/2 tbsp caster sugar
10ml/2 tsp lemon juice

1 Preheat the oven to 190°C/375°F/ Gas 5. Grease a 30 × 20cm/12 × 8in Swiss roll tin. Whisk together the egg yolks and caster sugar in a large bowl until the mixture is pale and the whisk leaves a trail when lifted. (The mixture should triple in volume.)

> — COOK'S TIP —
>
> An ideal way of serving the citrus ricotta squares is with seasonal soft fruits such as blackberries, peaches or apricots, soaked in a little cherry brandy (*maraska*).

2 Fold the hot water into the egg yolks, together with the flour and baking powder. Lightly whisk the egg whites in a grease-free bowl and then fold these into the egg yolks.

3 Pour the sponge mixture into the prepared tin, tilting it to help ease the mixture into the corners. Bake for 15–20 minutes, or until golden brown and firm to the touch. Turn out and cool on a wire rack, then carefully slice in half horizontally.

4 Make the filling by beating the ricotta cheese in a bowl and then stirring in the cream, caster sugar and lemon juice. Spread the filling on top of the base sponge then top with the remaining sponge half. Press down lightly on the top layer.

5 Chill the cake for 3–4 hours. Just before serving dredge with a little icing sugar and decorate with the lemon rind. Cut into 16 squares and serve with fresh fruit.

Baked Peaches

This Bulgarian recipe uses fresh peaches with a hint of cloves to give an aromatic, spicy flavour. Peaches are plentiful in summer so they are either dried, used in wines or brandy, or bottled to preserve them for use later on.

INGREDIENTS

Serves 6

40g/1½ oz/3 tbsp unsalted butter
6 firm ripe peaches, washed
12 whole cloves
90g/3½ oz/½ cup vanilla sugar
45ml/3 tbsp brandy or dry white
   wine (optional)
pistachios, mint leaves and a little sifted
   icing sugar, to decorate
whipped cream, to serve

1 Preheat the oven to 180°C/350°F/ Gas 4. Spread half the butter around an ovenproof dish, making sure both the sides and base are well coated.

2 Halve the peaches and remove the stones. Place the peaches skin side down in the dish. Push a whole clove into the centre of each peach half.

3 Sprinkle with the sugar and dot the remaining butter into each peach half. Drizzle over the brandy or wine, if using. Bake for 30 minutes, or until the peaches are tender.

4 Serve the peaches, hot or cold, with freshly whipped cream, pistachio nuts and sprigs of mint, and sprinkle with a little icing sugar.

Halva

Halva is the name for a sweetmeat or commercial sugar confectionery made throughout the Balkans. It can be based on wheat flour, cornmeal, semolina or rice flour with different proportions of butter, milk, water and sugar. If you are new to *halva*, this is a good basic version to start off with.

INGREDIENTS

Serves 6–8

275g/10oz/1½ cups fine-grained
   semolina
50g/2oz/4 tbsp butter
50g/2oz/¼ cup caster sugar
750ml/1¼ pints/3 cups very hot milk
grated rind of 1 lemon
90g/3½ oz/½ cup walnuts, chopped
chopped walnuts and halved
   pistachios, to decorate
cinnamon, for sprinkling

1 Dry fry the semolina carefully in a very heavy saucepan over a gentle heat for about 5 minutes, stirring continuously, or until the mixture turns a golden colour. Do not let it brown. Remove from the heat and add the butter and sugar, stirring until melted.

—— COOK'S TIP ——

Take care when dry frying the semolina so it does not burn on the base of the pan.

2 Return to a low heat and gradually add the milk to the pan, mixing well between each addition. Simmer for 5 minutes, then stir in the lemon rind and walnuts.

3 Simmer for 5 more minutes, stirring all the time, until very thick. Cover and leave for 2–3 minutes.

4 Fluff up the mixture with a fork. Serve warm, decorated with walnuts, pistachios and cinnamon.

Balkan Doughnuts

These flour-based doughnuts are a natural extension of the Eastern European love for dumplings. They are also the ideal showcase for home-made jam and are usually filled with a thick fruity jam, such as cherry, plum or apricot. Ideally, eat the doughnuts on the day of making.

INGREDIENTS

Makes 10–12
225g/8oz/2 cups strong flour, warmed
2.5ml/½ tsp salt
7g/¼oz sachet easy-blend dried yeast
1 egg, beaten
60–90ml/4–6 tbsp milk
15ml/1 tbsp granulated sugar
about 60ml/4 tbsp cherry jam
oil, for deep-fat frying
50g/2oz/¼ cup caster sugar
2.5ml/½ tsp cinnamon

1 Sift the flour into a bowl with the salt. Stir in the yeast. Make a well and add the egg, milk and sugar.

2 Mix together well to form a soft dough, adding a little more milk if necessary, to make a smooth, but not sticky, dough.

3 Beat well, cover with clear film and leave for 1–1½ hours in a warm place to rise until the dough has doubled in size.

4 Knead the dough on a lightly floured surface and divide it into 10–12 pieces.

5 Shape each into a round and put 5ml/1tsp of jam in the centre.

6 Dampen the edges of the dough with water, then draw them up to form a ball, pressing firmly to ensure that the jam will not escape during cooking. Place on a greased baking sheet and leave to rise for 15 minutes.

7 Heat the oil in a large saucepan to 180°C/350°F, or until a 2.5cm/1in piece of bread turns golden in 60–70 seconds. Fry the doughnuts fairly gently for 5–10 minutes, until golden brown. Drain well on kitchen paper.

8 Mix the caster sugar and cinnamon together on a plate or in a polythene bag and use to liberally coat the doughnuts.

Crescent Walnut Rolls

It is believed that the flaky dough used today to make croissants originated in the Balkan regions many years ago. The dough was filled with fruit or nut mixtures before being rolled up into crescent shapes.

INGREDIENTS

Makes 6
275g/10oz/1½ cups strong plain
   white flour, warmed
7g/¼oz sachet easy-blend dried yeast
40g/1½oz/3 tbsp vanilla caster sugar
very finely grated rind of 1 lemon
1 small egg, well beaten
40g/1½oz/3 tbsp unsalted
   butter, melted
120ml/4fl oz/½ cup warm milk
2 small egg yolks
granulated sugar, for sprinkling

For the filling
115g/4oz/1 cup walnuts,
   finely ground
5ml/1 tsp cinnamon
50g/2oz/¼ cup vanilla caster sugar
2 small egg whites

1 Warm the mixing bowl before sifting in the flour and stir in the yeast. Make a well in the centre of the flour and stir in the vanilla sugar, lemon rind, egg, melted butter and milk.

2 Knead well, adding a little extra liquid or flour if necessary to make a smooth, but not sticky, dough.

3 Knead the dough lightly on a lightly floured surface. Roll out thinly to a rectangle, about 45 × 30cm/ 18 × 12in; cut into 6 squares.

4 Mix the walnuts, cinnamon and sugar and egg whites. Divide among the squares, leaving a gap around the edges.

5 Carefully roll up each square diagonally, from one corner to the other, to form a long roll.

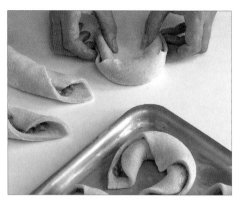

6 Curl the rolls into crescent shapes and place on a greased baking sheet. Leave in a warm place to rise, covered with clear film. This can take 1½–2 hours because the dough is rich.

7 Preheat the oven to 160°C/325°F/ Gas 3. Mix the egg yolks together and use a pastry brush to rub the yolks over the pastries. Cook for 15-25 minutes, or until golden. Remove from the oven and cool on a wire rack. Sprinkle with sugar before serving.

Bird of Paradise Bread

This Bulgarian bread, enriched with eggs and cheese, is named after its traditional decoration.

INGREDIENTS

Serves 10–12

15ml/1 tbsp dried yeast
60ml/4 tbsp lukewarm water
350g/12oz/3 cups flour, sifted
7.5ml/1½ tsp salt
90ml/6 tbsp natural yogurt
5 eggs, beaten
75g/3oz/⅓ cup feta cheese or *brinza*, finely chopped
15ml/1tbsp milk

For the topping

115g/4oz *kashkaval* or Cheddar cheese, sliced into 4 triangles
thick piece of ham, cut into 4 × 2.5cm/1in squares
4 pitted black olives (optional)
about 2.5cm/1in star shape cut out of red pepper

1 Sprinkle the dried yeast over the warm water in a small bowl. Leave to stand for 2–3 minutes, stir well then leave for 5–10 minutes until frothy.

2 Sift the flour and salt into a bowl. Make a well in the centre and pour in the yeast mixture, natural yogurt, 4 of the eggs and the feta cheese or *brinza*. Stir well together to form a dough, adding a little extra flour if necessary. Knead well on a lightly floured surface for about 10 minutes.

3 Shape the dough into an even ball, cover with clear film and leave in a warm place to rise until doubled in size, about 2 hours.

4 On a lightly floured surface gently knead the dough again and shape into a round to fit in a greased 20cm/8in springform tin, or place directly on a lightly buttered baking sheet. In a bowl, beat the 1 remaining egg with the milk and brush liberally over the loaf.

5 To decorate the loaf, arrange the cheese triangles evenly over the top to form a square in the middle. Place the ham and olives, if using, in between the cheese and put the star of red pepper in the centre. Leave to rise for about another 30–45 minutes. Preheat the oven to 200°C/400°F/Gas 6, then bake the loaf for 15 minutes.

6 Reduce the temperature to 180°C/350°F/Gas 4 and cook for a further 30–40 minutes, or until golden brown. Cool on a wire rack.

Mamaliga Bread

Mamaliga, or cornmeal, is one of the basic staple ingredients of the Balkan area. Cheese can be added to this light golden bread to give it a savoury taste.

INGREDIENTS

Makes 1 loaf or 9 small buns
75g/3oz/²⁄₃ cup self-raising flour
7.5ml/1½ tsp baking powder
75g/3oz/³⁄₄ cup cornmeal
2.5ml/½ tsp salt
1 egg
150ml/¼ pint/²⁄₃ cup milk
25g/1oz/¼ cup Cheddar cheese,
  finely grated (optional)

1 Preheat the oven to 200°C/400°F/ Gas 6. Place the self-raising flour, baking powder, cornmeal and salt into a large mixing bowl. Mix well, then make a well in the centre.

2 Add the egg, milk and Cheddar cheese, if using. Mix well with a wooden spoon.

3 Pour the mixture into a greased 15cm/6in round cake tin or a 9-hole bun tin.

4 Bake for 20–25 minutes or until well risen, golden and firm to the touch. Cool briefly on a wire rack. Serve warm in thick slices.

———— COOK'S TIP ————

Cook this loaf immediately after making, otherwise the raising agent will be less effective and the loaf will not be so light.

INDEX